CRITIC OF CRISIS

JAN GORAK

CRITIC OF CRISIS

A STUDY OF FRANK KERMODE

A LITERARY FRONTIERS EDITION, NO. 30

UNIVERSITY OF MISSOURI PRESS

COLUMBIA, 1987

Library of Congress Cataloging-in-Publication Data
Gorak, Jan, 1952–
  Critic of crisis: A Study of Frank Kermode.

  (A Literary frontiers edition)

  1. Kermode, Frank, 1919–   —Criticism and interpretation.
I. Title. II. Series.
PN75.K47G67   1985 801'.95'0924   86–30792
ISBN 0–8262–0634–4 (alk. paper)

⊗™ This paper meets the minimum requirements of
the American National Standard for Permanence of Paper
for Printed Library Materials, Z39.48, 1984.

TO IRENE

Contents

I. INTRODUCTION

IN nearly forty years as a literary critic, Frank Kermode has written on almost every conceivable topic and has employed almost every available critical method. His publications reveal a daunting range of interests, including Spenser, Shakespeare, and Chapman; Wells, Forster, Ford, Bennett, Gissing, Garnett, and Gerhardie; Spark, Murdoch, Bainbridge, and Colette; Henry Vaughan, Henry Fielding, Henry James, Henry Miller, and *Henry VIII*; Kenneth Tynan, Jack Kerouac, Bob Dylan, and student revolt; the 1964 Shakespeare centenary and the 1964 General Election; the New Testament and the new novel; Leavis, Empson, Richards, Tate, Sartre, Barthes, Foucault, Lionel Trilling, Mario Praz, Graham Hough, and Edmund Wilson. For breadth of interests and volume of output, Wilson serves, indeed, as Kermode's chief modern counterpart. Both critics share a special interest in the modern, and both have looked in unlikely places to sustain it. Yet a signal difference exists between them: where Wilson is a born analyzer, always ready to point out patiently the main lines of force in a new movement or major author, Kermode remains an unrepentant synthetist. One would not look to Kermode for an overview of E. M. Forster's literary career; but if one needed an essay showing his representative qualities as a typically modern specimen, then Kermode's "Forster" (1980) would seem ideal. If Wilson is the historian of modernity, Kermode is perhaps its typologist.

In 1963, Kermode observed, "Somebody should write a history of the word modern."[1] Kermode has devoted a long and often circuitous career to an understanding of the modern in its many manifestations. This book shows that the question of modernity stands at the very center of his work, dictating its subjects and con-

1

trolling its procedures. Even in his early days as a Renaissance scholar, Kermode showed a special eye for the modern. In editing *The Tempest* (1954), he fell upon a play that took as its immediate source the *Bermuda Pamphlets* describing the discovery of a new world. And when he began to collect material for a book on Spenser that never appeared, he chose for himself a poet almost as dark as the moderns themselves, whose greatest work he audaciously compared to Joyce's *Ulysses*.

At this time, when Kermode's work enjoys unprecedented prestige and controversy, it may be useful to review the shape of his career and its major preoccupations. Do his range and variety conceal a bookman's immersion in the topical, an eagerness to devour any new subject? Or do his diverse pursuits shape into more constant concerns and preoccupations? Is Kermode, as Jonathan Arac has respectfully described him, a critic we must confront "if we want to know where we are now," or does the bulk of his work conceal, as Gerald Graff has alleged, "the cheerful endorsement of ideas that, if taken seriously, would undermine the values he himself seems to stand for"?[2] Or does the truth lie rather in Frank Lentricchia's sketch in *After the New Criticism* (1980) of a critic who spent the 1960s trying to rebuild the ruins of New Critical theory into a less doctrinaire poetics, only to be overwhelmed by a flood of structuralists and deconstructors? Does his career, taken as a whole, reveal the seriousness and the consistency one expects from a major critic?

In Britain at least some eminent critics thought not. After the publication of *The Sense of an Ending* (1967), the book that consolidated Kermode's intellectual reputation, Graham Hough remarked on a curious insubstantiality in his achievement: "he began his literary career by writing a brilliant essay, and he is still writing brilliant essays. We are so much in his debt for original and suggestive ideas that we should like to be further indebted for the thorough and radical critical work that more than any one else in England he is capable of

2

writing."[3] More recently, Helen Gardner saw in Kermode's *The Genesis of Secrecy* (1979) "a brilliant and lively series of lectures" that remained ultimately unrewarding. Dame Helen linked Kermode with an influential contemporary movement that marked "a real loss of belief in the value of literature and literary study."[4] In recording the vicissitudes of the modern, she argued, Kermode had capitulated to the contemporary.

Blake Morrison has showed how early Kermode's grip on the contemporary began. In 1951, along with A. Alvarez, Kingsley Amis, F. W. Bateson, C. S. Lewis, J. R. R. Tolkien, and others, Kermode became one of the subscribers to John Wain's *Mixed Feelings*, the earliest vehicle for "The Movement."[5] Since then his grip has scarcely relaxed. His writing has appeared in *Twentieth Century, Spectator, New Statesman, London Magazine, Listener, Guardian, Salmagundi, Partisan Review, Raritan Review, Kenyon Review, New Review, New Literary History, Critical Inquiry, New York Times Book Review,* and *New York Review of Books.* For a brief and controversial period, Kermode coedited *Encounter*; and in 1979 he helped to found the *London Review of Books.* He has broadcast for the BBC and British Channel Four; he has served on the British Arts Council; and, perhaps most significantly of all, he has acted for the last sixteen years as general editor of the *Modern Masters* series.

Such credentials promote suspicion as well as awe. Can Kermode be as varied as such a list implies and remain critically sound? To pose such a question is to overlook his kinship with a distinctive phenomenon in modern letters, the tribe of bookmen who count writers like George Saintsbury, Leslie Stephen, Frederic Harrison, and, in recent times, Edward Garnett, Arnold Bennett, and Edmund Wilson among their numbers. All these writers combined literary expertise with what might almost be called cultural rapacity. They educated their audience in public; they reported on cultural developments abroad; they reflected on larger movements in a thoughtful and considered way; they sometimes encouraged new talents and usually treasured old; they were devoted to letters as an enterprise with a kind of catholicity, which, if it led them sometimes to an immersion in the second- or third-rate, at least gave them a sense of the universe of culture that more specialized critics can rarely enjoy. Moreover, the bookmen enjoyed an opportunity denied the professional critic of today. Constantly submerged in primary sources, they conducted their own educations right before the eyes of their readers. The whole life work of each took on the shape of intellectual autobiography, a genre that contemporary conditions have thrust to the middle or to the end of a critic's career.

One of the first requisites for a bookman is an opinionated curiosity, an ability to settle and to salvage reputations. Kermode has performed these duties well: his demolition of Peter Brook's *US* (*Encounter*, 1968) and his lengthy revaluation of the later William Golding (*New York Review of Books*, 1964) exhibit all the bookman's public intelligence. So too do many of his other essays on controversial movements and figures. Kermode was one of the first British critics to review Roland Barthes and perhaps the first to take Marshall McLuhan seriously. When Christopher Ricks fulminated in the *Listener* against student revolt, Kermode examined the argument both sympathetically and critically. If he thought that the 1960s had brought to prominence too many self-elected visionaries—Burroughs, Kerouac, Emmett Williams—he nonetheless spent some of the 1970s interviewing them in a bid to provide British readers with a sketch map of the latest new wave. As a bookman in an electronics age, Kermode has often moved beyond books, to present new movements in music, television, drama, cinema, and urban protest to a transatlantic public.

But in a period of self-conscious modernity, where the myth of perpetual revolution passes as orthodoxy in so many cultural circles, the bookman's role becomes a risky one. John Gross has shown how the massive in-

4

dustry of the Victorian and Edwardian bookman depended on privileges that no contemporary critic can enjoy. Without the benefits of the large, basically conservative audience of a Gosse or a Saintsbury, without the unprecedented revolution in literary techniques that Garnett and Wilson were able to mediate, the bookman may be reduced to inventing novelties or to defending shopworn orthodoxies. The career of Edmund Wilson, who was the subject of successive academic attacks, in 1948 by Stanley Hyman, in 1967 by Frederick Crews, and in 1977 by Marvin Mudrick, testifies to the endangered life of the postwar bookman. It is scarcely surprising to see so few distinguished contemporary practitioners; perhaps Richard Poirier, Denis Donoghue, and Christopher Ricks, in their varying ways, provide Kermode's only associates in the trade. Still more unpromisingly, developments in the marketplace have worsened the bookman's conditions of service: fewer and fewer journals pay for contributions, and their audiences dwindle almost by the day.

For this reason, the academy has become the bookman's second home, a profitable and attractive supplement to the pages of the magazines. Kermode's own academic career has certainly served him well. To list his record here is to unfurl a roll of honor. After gaining the John Edward Taylor Chair of English Literature at Manchester in 1958 at the age of thirty-nine, he has held a succession of distinguished professorships at Bristol, London, Cambridge, Jerusalem, Wesleyan, and Columbia, Lionel Trilling's alma mater. What better place than the academy for the critic who wants to understand the modern historically? If Kermode's literary journalism has allowed him direct access to the new, then his position in the academy has allowed him to detach himself from topicality so as to relate new to old. The "essay" that brought Kermode critical fame, *Romantic Image* (1957), exposed the romantic premises beneath modern poetics. At a time when A. Alvarez's *The Shaping Spirit* (1958) presented Wallace Stevens as operating at a hinterland of ordinary language, Kermode's own book two years later demonstrated Stevens's lines of descent from Coleridge and Wordsworth on the one hand and the meditative tradition on the other. Kermode's next controversial book, *The Sense of an Ending* (1967), discovered beneath the modern sense of crisis the imagery and the expectations of Christian apocalypse. Yet this passion for setting the present alongside the past does not turn Kermode into a conservative. On the contrary, when *The Classic* (1975) argued the power of classical tradition to accommodate Roland Barthes, many critics thought Kermode had ransomed the old to propitiate the new. (It is interesting to note that a portion of the book appeared in *New Literary History* as "A Modern Way with the Classic.") Yet Kermode has not shifted course. In *The Genesis of Secrecy* (1979), he compared Mark's *Gospel* to the *nouveau roman* in its abrupt inexplicitness, while in *The Art of Telling* (1983), he saw the *nouveau roman* itself as a successor to the romances of Chrétien de Troyes, since both kinds of narrative required readers "to work on the texts and supply meanings to them."[6]

Kermode's passion for continuity probably arises from his own early experience of the schisms and the crises in which modern history abounds. In a revealing memoir of Peter Ure, he describes how his youthful immersion in the great moderns yielded to the degrading circumstances of war. Those horrific years from 1940 to 1946 produced a schism in Kermode's personal life that he came to see as more widely representative of the modern experience of crisis. This experience accounts for his suggestion in 1963 that the history of the word *modern* might begin with a discussion of the fifteenth-century religious movement *devotio moderna*, which was characterized by a "sharp sense of epoch, and of reaction against the style of life and thought of immediate predecessors" (*CS*, 27). Modernity proceeds by a series of schisms, with the promise of an even greater schism always threatening to form its climax and its terminus.

Certainly, such a philosophy underpins the thought of the most influential moderns, Yeats, Eliot, Hulme, and Pound. Yet Kermode himself, of course, acted very much in the modern spirit when he refused to accept their explanations and revealed the paucity of historical evidence for the "myths of catastrophe" they advanced.

Kermode's desire to avoid the chimera of total explanations led him to develop an instrument more suited to understanding the shape of modern experience. Helped by the work of Nietzsche, Hans Vaihinger, I. A. Richards, and Wallace Stevens, he advanced the idea of the fiction, a provisional form of explanation akin to the scientific model, at its least a problem-solving mechanism, at its highest a road to insight. Instead of explaining all phenomena with reference to a grand mythical plot, a fiction proceeds by trial and error. Fictions are relative where myths are absolute, and they can be abandoned when they become obsolete. If the need for fictions in a reality that offers little sense of order remains constant, then the fictions themselves are disposable. Fiction is more characteristic of modernity than myth, since fiction participates in the sense of change and the willingness to question accepted categories that Kermode sees as indispensable to the modern frame of mind.

Kermode's endorsement of the fiction as a model to make sense of modernity has proved to be one of the most controversial aspects of his work, for it implies a relinquishing of the authority that critics from Arnold to Eliot have always taken for granted. But Kermode sees his position as a pluralistic one, whereby the critic retains his own values at the same time as he acknowledges the presence of very different ones. In the late 1960s, at the peak of student disorder in the United States, Kermode told *Partisan Review* readers, "We have no imperial rights over the culture, only the right to argue by whatever means we choose that our thing is worth doing."[7] Yet Kermode's opponents have argued that pluralism inevitably buckles into a kind of skeptical relativism that makes principled discussion impossible. Gerald Graff, among others, would count Kermode with Paul de Man and J. Hillis Miller as the type of critic who insidiously implies "that historical conditions compel us to accept the view the critic wishes us to accept."[8] Graff presents a difficult case for these critics to answer, for he suggests that their own professed pluralism may be as imperialist as the views they hope to dislodge.

Partly in answer to these criticisms, Kermode has for many years conducted an inquiry into the theory of narrative. The very structure and texture of narrative, he argues, will exhibit the kind of plurality that he himself has always valued. The history of the novel he sees as a history of anti-novels, of fictions abandoned in the pursuit of more complex representations of reality. Yet the history of narrative emerges as a history of accommodations rather than of schisms. Each kind of narrative elicits its own "form of attention" (the phrase, borrowed from Henry James, is a favorite of Kermode's), whether it be the layman's pursuit of the story or the interpreter's search for illumination. Narratives can accommodate both types of scrutiny, as the history of twentieth-century fiction has shown. Narrative, by virtue of its length, offers the kind of structured indeterminacy that modern audiences, with their competing desires for form and freedom, can thrive on. By drawing on E. H. Gombrich's work on the psychology of representation, Kermode has pointed to the reader's share in the generation of a narrative. Typically, he has refused to limit this share to the twentieth-century novel, reaching back through George Eliot and Henry Fielding in order to demonstrate a universal narrative potential.

Such a sustained inquiry into modern images and forms, when coupled with a complementary drive to relate these to what preceded them, clearly calls for unusual powers of speculation and synthesis. Kermode's own characterization of I. A. Richards as "a great borrower"[9] could well describe his own procedures. Kermode has borrowed the idea of "making sense" from Gombrich, the pattern of *figura* from Erich Auerbach, and the category of modern primitivism from Yvor Winters. He went to Ernst Kantorowicz for an account of Christian kingship and empire and served his apprenticeship in the history of ideas under Arthur Lovejoy. His later work on narrative theory and interpretation has clearly been inspired by Roland Barthes, while his discussion of "tacit knowledge" derives from Michael Polanyi.

How better to master modernity than to go to school with the best of the modern masters? Yet, like Richards, Kermode emerges as inimitably his own man. If he borrows the idea of the king's two bodies from Kantorowicz, he transforms this legal fiction into an existential lie when he shows its operation at the climax of *King Lear*, as the king insists on his divinity at the height of his insanity. Kermode borrows the idea of *figura* from Auerbach, but he repays the loan by enriching the meaning. Auerbach ended his discussion of the semantic development of the term at the beginning of the modern world in Dante, where "the literal meaning or historical reality of a figure stand in no contradiction to its profounder meaning, but precisely 'figures' it; the historical reality is not annulled, but confirmed and fulfilled by the deeper meaning."[10] But Kermode pushes Auerbach's *figurae* into a wholly secular modern world, where they point to a fulfillment that, however much our expectations might desire it, reality cannot grant. For Kermode, the *figura* embodies the deep rage for fulfillment that modern reality cannot provide. The same impulses motivate his reorientation of the history of ideas, where he transforms Lovejoy's analytical and philosophical discipline into an instrument for probing a series of key ideas of crisis (apocalypse, catastrophe, decadence) to which the modern mind has attached itself. Kermode shows T. S. Eliot's ability to borrow an idea and then present it with his own oblique grandeur.

Insofar as we can treat a text as not referring to what is outside or beyond it, we more easily understand that it has internal relationships independent of the coding procedures by which we may find it transparent upon a known world. . . . No one, however special his point of vantage, can get past all those doorkeepers into the shrine of the single sense. I make an allegory, once more, of Kafka's parable. . . . The pleasures of interpretation are henceforth linked to loss and disappointment, so that most of us will find the task too hard . . . and . . . slip back into the old comfortable fictions of transparency, the single sense, the truth.[11]

Kafka, Saussure, Starobinski, Levi-Strauss, Barthes, Philip Larkin (those "long perspectives" that "link us to our losses"): Kermode creates a disturbing harmony from some of the most spectral of modern voices.

Whatever the differences between Eliot's Anglican orthodoxy and Kermode's skeptical relativism, the poet probably remains his most decisive modern master. Despite Kermode's avowed affiliations to secrecy and to Stevens, it is the public and episcopal Eliot to whom he bears the strongest resemblance. In the accidents of publication and across the larger shape of a career, the two men share remarkable similarities. Both promise unpublished books (Eliot's *The School of Donne*, *The Outline of Royalism*, and *The Principles of Modern Heresy* match Kermode's projected book on Spenser and his *Modern Primitivism*). Both have remedied these omissions by collecting essays that hint at more organized systems of knowledge in a few suggestive paragraphs. Kermode's essays on Durrell, for instance, like Eliot's on Baudelaire, conceal a latent theory of modernity; neither writer spells out the full drift of his argument. In later life, both Kermode and Eliot took to the lectern, a venue that offers striking opportunities. In the guise of informality, the lecturer can issue powerful edicts (as when Eliot's *After Strange Gods* issues bans on the heretics, or when Kermode's "On Reading Novels" appears to encourage them). The lecture theater allows for great audacities, which can then be excused as ways, as Kermode has put it, "to make suggestions, to initiate discussion."[12] Both writers have used the lecturer's prerogative to dazzling effect.

Most important of all, both writers recognize crisis as the root condition of modernity, and both look to tradition as the chief means to assuage it. But Eliot's remains a tradition of empire that leads in one unbroken line of descent from Virgil and Dante to Eliot himself. Kermode refuses to accept a tradition that has played at least some part in two major twentieth-century wars. For Kermode, the imperial tradition forms part of the modern crisis; it cannot resolve it. No wonder that he has spoken so trenchantly of Philip Larkin's "poetry of constriction."[13] Out of his deep sense of the areas of constriction in modern experience, Kermode has built up a system of criticism emphasizing constraint at the level of commitment, liberty at the level of interpretation. Displaying Larkin's chastened expectations and sardonic skepticism, he has forged alliances with unstriking figures like Flacius, the sixteenth-century scholar who preserved the Bible from rival extremists; Forster, who reconciled the avant-garde novel to the expectations of his public; and Stevens, who accommodated his aestheticism to the routine of a corporate bureaucracy. Kermode's tradition owes its allegiances to the only empire left, the empire he sees in the text itself, which represents "the *imperium* to a full citizenship of which we hopelessly aspire: an *imperium* distorted in the transmission, subject to outrageous claims, but in the long run still there, indeed *sine fine*."[14] Kermode testifies to the virtue of continuity in a most tentative fashion; continuity and change provide the poles between which his distinctive critical idiom consistently moves.

II. THE IMAGE

THE publication of *Romantic Image* in 1957 marked the appearance of the man Joseph Frank called "the most interesting and provocative analyst of modernism in English."[1] Kermode certainly packed much provocative matter into this short essay of just over one hundred and fifty pages, which he described, challengingly enough, as "revising historical categories."[2] His most categorical revision turned on the relationship between nineteenth- and twentieth-century literature. By examining the dominant aesthetic assumptions of each period, Kermode sought to prove that both shared a belief in the saving grace of "the Image as a radiant truth out of space and time, and in the necessary isolation or estrangement of men who can perceive it" (*RI*, 13). Such a belief governed the iconography of the poems and the characteristic concerns of the major poets in both periods. The effect of Kermode's reorientation, as the *TLS* reviewer pointed out, was to show "that the modern movement in English poetry, the movement of revolt which we associate with the names of T. E. Hulme, Mr. Ezra Pound, Mr. T. S. Eliot, the later work of Yeats, is not a reversal of the Romantic tradition, but, like that French Symbolist tradition of which Valéry was the last great ornament, the logical continuer of it."[3]

Not all reviewers appeared convinced by this controversial argument, however. M. H. Abrams warned readers of *Victorian Studies* that Kermode's synthesis was audacious but inaccurate: "As a history of critical theory . . . *Romantic Image* must be read with caution. In the zeal and specialty of his interest the author sometimes converts his working hypothesis into a thesis for special pleading. . . . Taken in their totality, in fact, the major Romantic theories of poetry are at the opposite pole from contemporary notions of the alien poet and the autonomous image."[4] Like Abrams, Donald Davie had to reject the larger historical picture Kermode offered. *Romantic Image* lumped together diverse poetic traditions from the romantics to the present, producing a history that Davie called "a dull dog indeed." Unable to understand the rehumanized symbolism of Eliot and Pound, unable to judge between the frigid brilliance of Mallarmé and the frigid banality of Lionel Johnson and Ernest Dowson, the book emerged as considerably less audacious than its own initial claims. Out of premises very different from Abrams's (he thought that Kermode suffered from a reluctance to make value judgments), Davie reached broadly similar conclusions: "What Mr. Kermode offers us as the poetry of our own times isn't after all a post-symbolist poetry but a poetry that is symbolist *tout court*."[5]

Does *Romantic Image* argue for historical continuity at the expense of historical change? In his zeal to demolish modernist assumptions about the romantic past, does Kermode capitulate to much more specialized assumptions about poetic alienation and aesthetic autonomy that the romantics would certainly have repudiated and which the moderns themselves only intermittently endorsed? To see Kermode's book as a belated symbolist manifesto or as a partisan history of aesthetic theory is, in fact, to underestimate the sheer variety of its procedures, interests, and aims. His investigation of the shared assumptions of nineteenth- and twentieth-century poets leads quite naturally into an analysis of the themes and the images that the poets shared. His attack on the kind of cultural history that posits a "dissociation of sensibility" leads him to recommend the deposed Milton to twentieth-century poets and, by implication, to redraw the entire New Critical canon. His interest in the basis of romantic and modern judgments supports his bid to understand the fluctuating reputation of John Donne and the significant misunderstandings that underpin his current prestige. His final pages, which expose the flaws in contemporary poetics and suggest a program of reform, rest on the historical and critical authority with which Kermode has conducted his previous discussion. *Romantic Image* could only have been written by a man of strong, long, and varied views.

The immediate inspiration of the book was, however, revisionary and polemical. In November and December 1956, Kermode broadcast two talks on BBC radio entitled "The Myth of Catastrophe." These talks demonstrate the controversial and anti-authoritarian impulses that were to underprop *Romantic Image*, as Kermode makes clear his aversion to a new orthodoxy about the Renaissance that sees only disaster in Renaissance humanism. Deriving from "Roman Catholic writers like Maritain or . . . Anglo-Catholic theologians," the new orthodoxy threatened to spread beyond the Renaissance to the very frontiers of the modern.

> The Renaissance, it is said, neglected the fact of original sin and that neglect makes impossible either art or life of any quality. Anthropocentric humanism, a disease which entered its most destructive phase with the Romantic glorification of personality, is responsible for most of our troubles—our acquisitiveness, our ethical chaos, even in the end our disrespect for the human personality. All our mess is the result of the secularism of the Renaissance. We live in a state of division, our own world a mere bundle of fragments; and so it has been since the great catastrophe of about A.D. 1500.[6]

As a student of the modern, Kermode has always had a keen eye for a catastrophe. Since the "great catastrophe" he describes here is alleged to have poisoned our personal relationships, distorted our relations with our recent past, and linked all history since A.D. 1500 into one secular chain of continuous decline, then the evidence for it warrants careful investigation. When Kermode found little evidence for such a catastrophe, he did not respond with indignation. Instead, he submitted the accounts of it to a more affective and functional inquiry. More interesting than whether the catastrophe actually happened was "the obvious attractiveness of the notion that there was one."[7] In Kermode's view, political and cultural history may have only intermittent connections. Cultural shifts, he implies, may have little purchase on objective reality; they may in fact bear much more resemblance to the poets' own retrospective projections. Kermode, in other words, questions the very ground on which cultural history is normally written—dogmatic and aesthetic ground, in his view, bearing almost no relation to historical events.

Kermode's broadcast displays much of the enthusiasm for heresy that later entered into *Romantic Image*. The same iconoclasm that enabled him to label a powerful modern orthodoxy as a myth propels the whole book as it proceeds to rout many a treasured critical shibboleth. Is it orthodoxy that modernism makes an impersonal step in the direction of order, a mature withdrawal from romantic effusion? Then Kermode will prove its debt at every turn to the romanticism it claims to have outgrown. Are there not significant affinities between seventeenth-century England and modern times? Kermode will show Eliot's Anglicans as the product of the same projections that inspired Montaigne's cannibals. Does modern criticism declare paraphrase heretical? Kermode will point to its incorrigibly periphrastic bent. Kermode's iconoclasm extends even to questions of method. In the foreword to his *The Finer Tone* (1953), Earl Wasserman offered a sardonic appraisal of the current conventions: "although most explicators are sensible men and know the need of reaching outside the text for information, it is clear that they resent the act, engage in a ritual of verbal self-flagellation for occasional transgressions, and wish the work of art were so self-sufficient it could not tempt them to sin."[8] Even so, Wasserman organized his own book as a set of readings of six poems. No similar compunctions affected John Wain two years later when he edited, in the manner of

Cleanth Brooks's *The Well Wrought Urn*, a whole volume of explications entitled *Interpretations*.

More venturesome than either critic, Kermode in *Romantic Image* repeatedly deplores the tedium of "another explication," turning instead to the *topos* of the dancer or the iconography of the tree. This invasion into the methods of the Warburg school perhaps lies behind his biting comment on the "deplorably specialised" skills of "dons these days" (Preface). The charge could hardly stick to the author of *Romantic Image*, who in the space of a single page sweeps from Ficino to Dürer to Burton and down from Coleridge, Shelley, and Keats to Yeats and to Celtic mythology. Kermode looks to Milton and Yeats as heroic liberators. The first is author of "the most perfect achievement of English poetry," and the critic looks forward to a time when "poets will marvel that it could have been done without so long; as easy, they will say, to imagine a Greek literature which abjured Homer" (*RI*, 181). This is Kermode as bookman: the caustic celebrant of a future that his own pen hopes to create, the critical equivalent of the prophetic Yeats, who "found his solution to that most urgent problem of discourse, assuming that such a statement as 'The best lack all conviction,' in contact with the vast image out of *Spiritus Mundi*, puts on the knowledge with the power of that image." The result is that "the slaves of time, the non-poets, will find a validity in his symbolic poems that is, for them, absent from the pure poetry of the dream. They share with the poet not only the Great Memory, but also the ordinary syntax of the daily life of action" (*RI*, 176). Kermode's prose takes on the same qualities it celebrates in Yeats. His tone moves from the forensic to the eulogistic, so that the advocate who reiterates the poet's achievements blends into the enthusiast who achieves redemption through his noble vision. And in his last pages, Kermode dons his most audacious mask of all, emerging not as an archaeologist who has come to recover a tradition but as a prophet who has come to bury one. "Somehow, and probably soon," he comments, "the age of dissociation . . . must end" (*RI*, 177).

*   *   *

For all its polemical vigor, *Romantic Image* remains a late addition to a second-wave "romantic revival" that began with Jacques Barzun's *Romanticism and the Modern Ego* (1943). Barzun moved energetically to defend the romantic movement against mounting charges of aesthetic confusion and political authoritarianism. He conducted his defense in terms that sought to establish the moral centrality of romanticism, remarking on the "creative mission" by which romantic writers perceived "a great contradiction concerning man. I mean the contrast between man's greatness and man's wretchedness; man's power and man's misery."[9] After Barzun's spirited moral and political defense, romantic research took a more theoretical turn. Two important scholarly works, M. H. Abrams's *The Mirror and the Lamp* (1953) and René Wellek's second volume of *A History of Modern Criticism* (1955), built the foundations on which a reassessment of the movement's aesthetic principles could be undertaken. In 1949, Cleanth Brooks's foreword to R. W. Stallman's *Critiques and Essays in Criticism* had spoken entirely seriously of a "romantic conception of poetry" that took "quite literally the view that poetry is the spontaneous overflow of emotion."[10] The appearance of these two books made such statements less credible and cleared the ground for a revaluation of the relationship between romantic and modern poetry and poetics.

By the publication of *Romantic Image* in 1957, several such reassessments had appeared. Herbert Read's *The True Voice of Feeling* (1953) demonstrated the importance of the organic metaphor for romantic authors, and even for professed anti-romantics like T. E. Hulme and Ezra Pound. Murray Krieger's *The New Apologists for Poetry* (1956) traced New Critical premises to their origins in the thought of Samuel Taylor Coleridge. Perhaps the most significant contribution to this movement, however, came in Robert Langbaum's *The Poetry of Experience* (1957), a book that reconciled Barzun's intellectual and moral concerns to the formal and aesthetic investigation that Abrams and Wellek had initiated. Langbaum saw romanticism as the central modern tradition, with "postenlightenment literature" from Wordsworth to the present as the product of a common predicament (a paralyzing self-consciousness), a common goal (the escape into experience), a common philosophy (relativism), and a common form (the dramatic monologue). Langbaum looked beyond the twentieth century's image of itself as a period "emancipated to the point of forlornness," emphasizing instead its affinities with the romantic "attempt to salvage on science's own empiric grounds the validity of the individual perception against scientific abstractions." Like Kermode, Langbaum had doubts about the authority of the tradition that early twentieth-century authors had erected. "Tradition is," he remarked, "the thing we have not got. . . . The word helps construct for us that image of ourselves which constitutes the modern pathos."[11] Under Langbaum's searchlight, tradition revealed itself less as a public corpus of accepted beliefs and values than as the idealized projections of anguished modern men. All the imposing machinery of modern literature—the hermetic mythologies, the cults of order, the neo-Christian resurgencies and counter-Renaissance crusades—counted for less than the basically valueless, meaningless world on which postenlightenment poets had vainly tried to impose their forms.

Kermode resembles Langbaum in his desire to stretch the provenance of "romantic" to its utmost temporal limits and to bring the twentieth century back into line with the nineteenth century. With self-conscious boldness, he remarks, "Throughout this essay I . . . use 'Romantic' in a restricted sense, as . . . beginning in the late years of the eighteenth century and not yet finished." He then characterizes the movement in a

18

manner that lends the paradox of "restricted sense" a further frisson. By "Romantic," he continues, he refers to the "high valuation placed during this period upon the image-making powers of the mind at the expense of its rational powers, and to the substitution of organicist for mechanistic modes of thinking about works of art" (*RI*, 56). Kermode allows "Romantic" to extend temporally, but, unlike Langbaum, he diminishes its frame of reference. Langbaum centers the romantic crisis in a gulf between fact and value that his artists attempt to penetrate through experience extended and temporal. Kermode acknowledges this schism, but characteristically he allows his artists to escape through "the image-making powers of the mind." Langbaum's writers risk exhaustion, Kermode's extinction. If both kinds of artist are estranged from society, the nature of their estrangement differs. Kermode's artists court oblivion, Langbaum's risk transgression. Langbaum's typical romantic is Faust, whom no social order can restrain; Kermode's is Axel, whom none can even engage. In both cases, the romantic artist repeatedly strains at the uncrossable boundary between art and life, securing his liberation only at the expense of existence itself. There remains, clearly, an unbridgeable gap between the two perspectives. Whereas the image-making powers of the artist are subject to sudden and unexpected withdrawal, the poetry of experience remains permanently renewable. The arc of Goethe's *Faust* is a whole life; poets in the tradition of the image cannot, as the careers of Coleridge, Pater, and Wilde make plain, hope for nearly so much.

But what precisely do the poets in this tradition mean by *image*? Kermode follows closely in their tracks and shows that they saw images as poems, parts of poems, and epiphanies by turns. But unlike an earlier critic of the image, Kermode does not see this confusion as a problem. "The very word 'image,'" C. Day Lewis wrote in his *The Poetic Image* of 1947, "has taken on, during the last fifty years or so, a mystical potency:

think what Yeats made of it." Lewis himself characterized the image in Wordsworthian terms, as, on the one side, an omnipresent device, not restricted to any particular type of poem, and, on the other, as a permanent occupant in the human mind, imparting an "affinity between external objects" and even a "kinship with everything that lives or has lived."[12] Instead of an incongruity between the image and ordinary experience, Lewis saw an affinity, a deep mythical core where the image affirms the artist's kinship with the whole chain of created being.

This underlying affinity, of course, is precisely what Kermode's image-makers cannot rely on. Their activity, on the contrary, rests on opposition: between image and discourse, organism and mechanism, experience and vision. Indeed, as Kermode points out, behind the entire tradition lies the view that places "'imagination' in an antithetical relationship with 'reality'" (*RI*, 15). It follows, then, that poets working in this tradition become exiles, estranged from a reality they had no part in making, and with their own special language drawn from the unconscious and the dream. Only a fool would translate a poet's version of "moral" into a marketplace code of conduct. The typical image-maker stands alone, ignored or reviled by his society and exhausted by his craft; his reward, an image comprehended by a dwindling few, draws on storehouses of consciousness that perpetually threaten to close.

But does this picture of the poetic craft add up to a tradition? On the face of it, a "tradition of the image" would seem a contradiction in terms. How can a succession of isolated artists, each working toward his own private epiphany, achieve the reciprocity implied by the word *tradition*? One of Kermode's most important achievements is to demonstrate the common stock of images that modern poets have employed and to find these images in places that critics working on narrower grounds have not cared to look. He tracks the images of the dancer and the tree back from Yeats through the decadent 1890s and the earnest Victorians to the early romantics, and thus he uncovers an occult scheme that runs beneath the authorized version of literary history. Modern literature, for all its influential disclaimers, stands revealed as deeply romantic in its images and its assumptions. A favorite ploy is to remark how Hulme would not have surprised Symons or to show Arnoldian assumptions at the heart of a dialogue by Wilde. Symons may not have felt surprised at this; Kermode's readers certainly did.

Even so, Kermode's method runs the risk of pushing similarity into identity, a process that distorts the treatment of individual poems and poets. These distortions increase the further Kermode ventures from the tradition of the *Symbolistes*. For instance, he sees the inhuman sacrifice and preterhuman beauty associated with the image crystallized in the appearance of Keats's Moneta as well as in the Salome who captivated Wilde, Symons, and Yeats. But as M. H. Abrams has pointed out, Kermode notices Moneta's face while ignoring her words, with their promise "that thou may'st understand aright, / I humanize my sayings to thine ear." Moneta addresses the narrator as a human being, not as a poet. Kermode's treatment of Wordsworth seems even more arbitrary. He tells us that Wordsworth's *Preface* of 1800 "allows a difference between poets and other men." Nine lines later this has translated into the assertion that "the poet is necessarily estranged" (*RI*, 22), a deduction that by no means follows from Wordsworth's initial proposition. "What is a Poet?" he asks in the same preface. "He is a man speaking to men: a man, it is true, endowed with more lively sensibility, more enthusiasm and tenderness, who has a greater knowledge of human nature, and a more comprehensive soul, than are supposed to be common among mankind." Wordsworth continues in this spirit for several pages. Far from being estranged from mankind, his poet suffers from an excess of genial spirits. And far from cultivating a language remote from the language of men, Wordsworth concedes that the poet's words "must often, in liveliness and truth, fall short of that which is uttered by men in real life, under the actual pressure of those passions, certain shadows of which the Poet thus produces."[13] These hardly sound like the sentiments of an alienated image-maker trapped in the torture chamber of his solitary craft.

Kermode habitually selects the part of a poem that proves his case and habitually ignores the evidence that might invalidate it. Yet at least the documents, in the form of the poems and the prefaces, exist independently of his interpretations. When, however, he goes a stage further and begins "ruthlessly abstracting" parts of Wilde's "The Critic as Artist" in order to expose "disguised similarities" (*RI*, 57) with other authors, the critic becomes a ventriloquist, feeding his artists with lines that will best fit his thesis: "I have deliberately, in the last paragraph or two, shifted the language from Wildean to Blakean, Coleridgean, Bergsonian, with a hint or two of more immediately fashionable ways of talking about images, because the point is that all make similar assumptions and contribute to the same discussion" (*RI*, 60). A similarity of terminology, however, does not automatically translate into an identity of assumption. How can Kermode assert that these writers "contribute to the same discussion" without giving a clearer sense of how that discussion progressed? What Wordsworth means by *poet* and Wilde means by *artist* can only become apparent after a full discussion of each. To select parts of Wordsworth on the basis of their resemblance to parts of Wilde and then to claim larger similarities of assumption between them is a procedure not without a certain circularity. The tactic of blending poets into an identikit picture of the image-maker takes for granted a likeness it was the critic's task to establish by proof. At no point does Kermode subject a nineteenth-century poem or preface to the detailed scrutiny he extends to Yeats. Like the symbolists themselves, he betrays an unwillingness to develop a continuous public discourse.

He wants his artists to float free of circumstance so that he can examine their verbal resemblances in glorious isolation.

What is the effect of this effort to recruit as many poets as possible for the tradition of the image? One result is that the aspirations of a wide range of poets become narrowed to one exclusive goal, the pursuit of the image. Kermode allows the image to dominate his sense of literary history: it caps the career of Yeats and explains the defections of Coleridge and Arnold. In Kermode's eyes, Arnold's career after the *Poems* of 1853 becomes a mistake, while the simple fact that Wordsworth continued writing important and influential works when the image had long deserted him is never confronted. As literary history, this hardly seems accurate; the nineteenth-century poets have been swept into a more strictly modern predicament. A second result is that Kermode manages to roll back the date of the modern crisis. If Keats and Wordsworth can be shown as isolated outcasts, then the estrangements of Yeats and Eliot become typical rather than extravagant. In fact, as Kermode tells it, a tradition of crisis had been established in English poetry as early as 1800.

*   *   *

Yet if Kermode extends one crisis he annihilates another. The most contentious part of his book emerges in the chapter "The Dissociation of Sensibility," as he tackles what Robert Stallman has called the "one basic theme in modern criticism." The phrase reached the British public through the mediation of T. S. Eliot, whose review of Sir Herbert Grierson's *The Metaphysical Poets* (1921) used it with reference to the mind of the modern poet. But, as Stallman remarks, the term quickly extended beyond the poet's loss of a "fixed convention" to the conviction of a "loss of tradition . . . loss of belief, loss of a world order." Yet, despite its wide currency, the idea remained too controversial to command unconditional acceptance. It began to lose its authority when Eliot's alliances with Church and with royalist State became overt. In 1929, Edmund Wilson's "T. S. Eliot and the Church of England" attacked the historical roots of the idea, seeing in Eliot's Anglo-Catholicism only a search for a pastoral idyll. Yvor Winters's *The Anatomy of Nonsense* (1943) echoed these criticisms while characteristically harshening them. After reviewing the historical ideas of Henry Adams, he remarked that "Adams' view of the Middle Ages, which has been adopted by Eliot and his followers, is merely a version of the Romantic Golden Age; the thirteenth century as they see it never existed." So far, the idea had remained safe in name at least. But in 1946, Bonamy Dobrée attacked it more directly, wondering whether the phrase was anything more than a slogan brandished by an "Anglo-Catholic movement seeking arguments to justify its attitude." Five years later, F. W. Bateson questioned its pedigree by exposing how Eliot had applied "to the nation Gourmont's analysis of the mental process of the individual." Although Bateson stopped short of considering the cultural ramifications of his argument, he had nonetheless delivered a decisive blow to the historicity of the idea.[14]

Kermode's contribution to the debate gained much praise from his reviewers. Graham Hough told *Encounter* readers of his "massive and devastating attack on the 'dissociation of sensibility' doctrine." The effect of the attack was to annihilate the machinery that "sets up Donne against Milton, sets up all poets of a supposedly unified sensibility against all poets of a supposedly dissociated one." Philip Larkin and Thom Gunn went even further, seeing Kermode's discussion as a liberating one, because it released contemporary poets from an authority that they did not choose to follow.[15]

Certainly, Kermode secures a rapid conviction. He moves from a very brief examination of T. S. Eliot's testimony, which he finds "attractive because it gave design and simplicity to history" (*RI*, 155), to an equally

24

drastic excursion through history. After a seven league leap from third-century Athens to seventeenth-century England, he concludes that no period of European history coincided with Eliot's description. From this evidence, he decides that "there was, in the twentieth [century], an urgent need to establish the historicity" of a crisis in the seventeenth century. His explanation becomes attractive in its simplicity: "The theory of the dissociation of sensibility is, in fact, the most successful version of a Symbolist attempt to explain why the modern world resists works of art that testify to the poet's special, anti-intellectual way of knowing truth" (*RI*, 158). Kermode alleges that the theory of dissociation has come into prominence because of the persuasive powers of image-makers themselves, and in this way he credits this group with an influence that the rest of his study has been indirectly devoted to subverting. Even so, his explanation has its problems. How did these isolated and alienated men convince so many of their audience to buy their propaganda at the same time as their poetry was ignored? The explanation makes no sense in terms of the sociology of art as *Romantic Image* presents it. Only Kermode's contention that the idea of dissociation drove certain poets from the canon seems fully persuasive. Helped by Joseph Duncan's scholarly article, "The Revival of Metaphysical Poetry, 1872–1912" (*PMLA*, 1953), Kermode has few problems in showing how Donne's boosted twentieth-century stock rests on the efforts of clerical editors like Alexander Grosart working in the nineteenth century, who saw Donne as a poet combining ratiocination and passion, intelligence and ardor in a difficult and sensuous poetry.

Milton lost ground because of the twentieth century's intensification of influential nineteenth-century prejudices in favor of the short poem. When these were added to the institutional preference for wit rather than sublimity that underpins critical statements like F. R. Leavis's *Revaluation* (1936) and Cleanth Brooks's *Modern Poetry and the Tradition* (1939), then clearly the new tradition had little room for Milton. Kermode makes great play with the unhistorical grounds for the reconstruction that modern criticism effects. The lives of neither poet will stand the projections the critics wish to foist on them. Donne was so afflicted by the New Philosophy that he ended his life as Dean of St. Paul's, while Milton was so incapable of integrating thought and feeling that he managed to write *Paradise Lost* and *De Doctrina Christiana*.

Kermode's explanation, however, that "powerful aesthetic interests were being satisfied by the conversion of a little-known poet into an English Laforgue" (*RI*, 164), remains much less convincing. Donne's modern reputation may have been created in these terms, but it could hardly have been so sustained. Indeed, the kinds of interest the poet served were just too broad to allow him to be fixed in a symbolist straitjacket. How did Donne become a talisman for F. R. Leavis, whose premises are hardly Laforguean? How did he attract William Empson, who never had a good word to say for symbolism? Eliot's comments in "The Metaphysical Poets" may have provided the initial stimulus for both these critics, who remained free to fashion a Donne according to their own specifications. At this point in his argument, Kermode sees images everywhere, wielding the idea as a crowbar to pry open every corner of literary history.

Similar reservations extend to Kermode's discussion of the cultural wing of the dissociationist doctrine, the search for a golden age of the image, a period of stability and harmony when poets lived, as Yeats put it, in "unity of being." By casting his net with his customary breadth, bringing into his discussion not just Eliot but also Hulme, not just Yeats but also Henry Adams, Kermode effectively stands the doctrine on its head. The evidence as he so wittily presents it does indeed make a farce of the concept. The lack of chronological unanimity becomes almost painful. Henry Adams plays a thirteenth-century age of unity against a twentieth-century age of multiplicity. Yeats and Hulme push the date of schism forward to 1450–1550. Eliot manages to delay it until 1642, the date of the English Civil War. At this stage, Kermode calls off the hunt, remarking that "a once-for-all-event cannot happen every few years; there cannot be, if the term is to retain the significance it has acquired, dissociations between the archaic Greeks and Phidias, between Catullus and Virgil, between Guido and Petrarch, between Donne and Milton" (*RI*, 161). It is as if a panel of distinguished historians were each to turn up different dates for the outbreak of the French Revolution. Kermode's conclusion, that the idea of cultural dissociation had its origins in the minds of poets rather than in the events of history, scarcely permits dispute.

But once again, his explanation for the phenomena he dissects proves more contentious. Can one really assume that Adams, Yeats, and Eliot all examined history from exactly the same perspective? To bracket Eliot's seventeenth-century England, "animated by a rich nostalgia for the great period of Anglican divinity" (*RI*, 156), alongside Hulme's cult of what E. H. Gombrich has called "the mystery-loving, eye-gouging Byzantines" is to conflate a myth of civility with a myth of order.[16] Similarly, Adams's Chartres answers to needs bearing more closely on conditions in industrial America than on any glorification of the image. Nor can the artists' historical sensibilities be altogether written off. A "once-for-all-crisis" may be too much to ask for; but upheavals of some importance may well have occurred in each of the periods cited. If, as Kermode tells us, scientists were persecuted in the England of Elizabeth I but were granted a Royal Society in the reign of Charles II, then this surely supports Eliot's point that "something . . . happened to the mind of England between the time of Donne or Lord Herbert of Cherbury and the time of Tennyson and Browning."[17] The impossibility of a Golden Age does not rule out the existence of great strains in the real one; the absence of a "once-for-all-crisis" does not rule out the possibility of one that made its way creepingly and insidiously.

Even so, one cannot find the same sort of evidence for a "dissociation of sensibility" as for the Battle of the Boyne. Kermode's discussion points to the need for a more sensitively tuned instrument to detect cultural shifts. Once developed, such an instrument would not so much demolish the idea of dissociation as include it among the phenomena to be investigated, as an idea that attached itself to a variety of interests over a period of time. In his overwhelming desire to clinch his case, Kermode does not submit the idea to patient scrutiny. Does the bookman in him overcome the historian? Once again, the conduct of his argument proves too polemical to support his own initial premises or even to answer to the examples he cites. Once he has decided to see dissociation as a primitivistic myth, Kermode can marshal his evidence to show that such a paradise never existed. But he has not proved conclusively his own major premise, that the idea did indeed constitute a form of primitivism. Like the writers he aims to correct, Kermode reads all history in terms of the image. His desire to fuse similarity of assumption into identity of end means that he does not so much demolish the concept of dissociation as diminish it.

*   *   *

In the last pages of *Romantic Image*, Kermode offers a program for contemporary poetry and poetics. He began his chapter on the dissociation of sensibility with the remark, "We shall never find a state of culture worth bothering about . . . in which language is so primitive as to admit no thinking that is not numinous" (*RI*, 157). Near the end of the chapter Kermode hopes that modern poetics will find a place for discourse, "the ordinary syntax of the daily life of action" (*RI*, 176). This hope, and the restoration of Milton by which Kermode, oddly enough, thought it might be effected, caused not a little critical confusion. M. H. Abrams thought Kermode's program consisted of a marriage between "the Symbolist poetic" and "an adequate semantics," while Joseph Frank saw him as arguing that the symbolist poetic "performed a noble function in its time, but its time has passed."[18]

The conflicting testimony about Kermode's intentions perhaps results from the immense uncertainty in these pages, which culminates in his praise of Milton in Yeatsian terms, as a poet who "'has found, after the manner of his kind, / Mere images'" (*RI*, 182). On the one hand, Kermode seems clear that the tradition of the image has bequeathed incorrigible contradictions to modern poetics. He points to the way that the poetic drive for images conflicts with the critic's duty to discourse. The poets in this tradition would all like to mint their own words. Critics, on the other hand, must always reduce vision to ordinary language. The complaint of T. E. Hulme, who deplored the tendency of words to "crawl along" and wanted "genius, music, to make them stand up," points to the dismay of the whole movement.[19] For once they dance to the image-maker's tune, words quickly become unfathomable, thus driving the poet further into estrangement. Hulme's *Speculations*, which read like a man conducting a furious argument with himself, betray the image-maker's impossible task. Hulme can never explain what he wants to do with poetic language without teetering over into absurdity of the sort his prose voice deplores.

Hulme's problem becomes endemic among his critical successors. Committed to a view of language as anti-discursive, anti-referential, dogmatically certain that paraphrase is a heresy and meaning achievable only within the poem as a whole, how does a critic in this tradition conduct his business? Kermode argues that much of the obscurity and the strenuousness of modern criticism comes as "a direct consequence of its Symbolist inheritance" (*RI*, 173). The theoretical statements of the New Critics, with their resolute insistence on the superiority of poetic language to scientific discourse, their persistent praise of paradox, and their dislike for plain statement, all derive from the tradition of the image.

Kermode wants to move modern poetics away from its obscurity and out of its belligerently defensive attitude to the marketplace and to science. He calls for a new poetics that would turn less on the absolute distinctions that have hardened into New Critical dogma than on a rapprochement between the language of science and the language of poetry. His own poetic at this point rests on a theory that would find "a different place for discourse from any found for it during the nineteenth-century . . . a waking poetic, respecting order" (*RI*, 175–76). In a corresponding call to poets, he recommends the restoration of *Paradise Lost*, "perhaps the richest and most intricately beautiful poem in the world" (*RI*, 181).

This is Kermode's program, and there is no denying its humane impulses. Yet his recommendations are full of inconsistencies. How can a criticism that for two centuries has marched resolutely under the banner of expression suddenly reverse itself and look to Milton as a model? Nor does it seem accurate to see any poetic sponsored by Eliot and Hulme as guilty of not "respecting order." Hulme at least appeared to respect it almost too much. What this poetic did lack, in its hectic concern with expression, was a corresponding concern with action and with imitation. When critics in this tradition turned their minds to audiences, they saw only an ideal fiction, an organic society of warriors or illiterate peasants. Kermode's revised poetic, which admits discourse in order to complicate the paradoxes of the image, remains more of an expansion of this tradition than a departure from it. In a revealing citation from Yeats, he suggests that Milton be readmitted to the canon as a finder of "images" (*RI*, 182). His closing pages give the impression of an author on the threshold of all sorts of new discoveries but for the moment unable to commit them to print.

III. FICTIONS

ROMANTIC *Image* marked Kermode's first confrontation with the schismatic and occult impulses of modern literature. The doctrine of the image tried to sever poetry from the life of action and contingency and to secure it for the realm of vision and unity. According to the doctrine, an apocalyptic crisis separated modern men from the past. This crisis threw artists into a world that in its fragmented disunity resembled a realm of anti-art. Yet, as Kermode's final remarks stressed, art had to take some account of this reality, since "art was always made *for* men who habitually move in space and time, whose language is propelled onward by verbs, who cannot always be asked to respect the new enclosure laws of poetry" (*RI*, 176–77). A poetics more congenial to temporality and contingency, more hospitable to the matter and the audience for art must surely be devised.

Kermode hoped that Milton might point toward this poetic. But the restored Milton of Harold Bloom's *The Visionary Company* (1961) appeared only as a benighted image-maker who "after the failure of his Revolution, turned inward like Oedipus, making of his blindness a judgment upon the light."[1] Such a restoration made imagination antithetical to reality, with literary history continuing to be composed according to crisis models. No restoration could be effected in these terms. However, the previous year Kermode made his personal bid toward the restoration of Milton by editing an essay-collection called *The Living Milton* (1960). As well as gathering together contributions from several distinguished younger critics, he offered his own assessment in a long essay called "Adam Unparadised." In particular, he tried to rescue the poet from the criticisms of doctrinal confusion and formal imperfection leveled against him in A. J. A. Waldock's *Paradise Lost and Its*

Critics (1947). Kermode began by a typically ingenious piece of lateral thinking. "Milton wrote a theological treatise," he commented, "but *Paradise Lost* is not it."[2] At the heart of the poem was no dour reassertion of orthodoxy but rather a great peripeteia that dramatized "the contrast between a world we can imagine, in which the senses are constantly and innocently enchanted, and a world of which this is not true" (*SSD*, 269). The poem worked mythically like *Ulysses*, not doctrinally like the *Summae*. In this way, by suggesting that the work owed more to Joyce than to Aquinas, Kermode made Milton new for another generation of readers.

Kermode reconstructed Milton largely in the light of his own current interests. In the decade between the publication of *Romantic Image* (1957) and *The Sense of an Ending* (1967), he returned repeatedly to the nature of myth and modernity, exploring these problems as a reviewer for some of the most important literary journals. Two influential critics he encountered during these years, the Canadian sages Northrop Frye and Marshall McLuhan, consolidated the tradition attacked in *Romantic Image*. Frye's *Anatomy of Criticism* (1957) clearly seemed inspired by the symbolist perception of art as a realm of purity and order. Kermode saw in Frye's work a golden dream of the past, "the fact of recurrence . . . the primitive mythical level of seasonal recurrence and rebirth."[3] McLuhan projected the same golden dream into the future; his *Understanding Media* (1964) looked to an electronic tribalism unleashed in the "global village" of the media. Kermode was enlightened, but unimpressed. Of Frye's *A Natural Perspective* (1965), he commented, "He is the critic of regress, writing regressive criticism about plays he finds to be regressive" (*CS*, 119). He identified similar regressions beneath McLuhan's *The Gutenberg Galaxy* (1963), a work that once again explained the modern crisis by reference to one significant event in the past. Kermode seemed skeptical whether the invention of the printing press could bear the kind of weight McLuhan put on it. Frye's myth of an undissociated past and McLuhan's myth of an undissociated future both seemed "ways of evading the terrors of actual history." More useful he suggested "to ask ourselves why at a moment like the present . . . we find such obvious comfort . . . in pseudo-historical explanations."4

During the late 1950s and the 1960s Kermode found such questions easier to pose than to resolve. The crucial question about the modern relationship to the past broached in the last pages of *Romantic Image* still awaited its answer. Meanwhile, an English quarrel of the period approached the question in a significantly different way. C. P. Snow's *The Two Cultures* (1959) pointed to a dangerous schism between scientists (who looked to the future) and cultural traditionalists (who looked to the past). The one group "have their future in their bones"; the other "responds by wishing the future did not exist."5 Three years later, in a Richmond lecture delivered at Downing College, Cambridge, F. R. Leavis answered Snow on behalf of what Snow had called "the traditional culture." Leavis accused Snow of ignorance. "He knows nothing of history," Leavis observed, and so has "no notion of the changes in civilisation that have produced his 'literary culture' and made it possible for C. P. Snow to enjoy a status of distinguished intellectual . . . and be (with practical consequences) an authority in the field of higher education: things that the real, the living 'traditional culture' (for there is a reality answering to that phrase) can no more countenance today [than] it could have foreseen them in the nineteenth century."6 Between the Snow who considered culture a matter of corporate unanimity and the Leavis who commandeered all the "human" values and the honorific terms for his own use, there could be no genuine dialogue. Kermode's review of *The Two Cultures* acknowledged that Snow left the humanities with a case to answer: "the cultural divide about which Sir Charles writes so well seems to me to reflect a grand modern antinomy" (*PE*, 29). But his silence in the noisy and unedifying debate that followed the appearance of Leavis's lecture is perhaps significant. His own answer would not appear until 1967 with the publication of *The Sense of an Ending*, where he would reject the schismatic premises of both parties in order to define the anxieties and the assumptions shared by past, present, and future, humanities and sciences alike.

In the United States another variant of the battle between past and future raged across generational lines. Leslie Fiedler, the Crèvecoeur of the younger generation, celebrated an American country of the young capable of mass producing its own ready-made myths. The long apprenticeships in art followed by Yeats, Valéry, and Joyce were superseded by the hallucinogenic intensities of Kesey, Burroughs, and Ginsberg. Instead of the religion of art, these authors endorsed the values of anti-art. Instead of shouldering the burden of the past, they erupted into the spontaneous epiphanies of the authentic present. In his *Waiting for the End* (1964), Fiedler opened hostilities by acting as spokesman for present and future. On the other side, Philip Rahv's *The Myth and the Powerhouse*, Lionel Trilling's *Beyond Culture*, and Edmund Wilson's *The Bit Between My Teeth* (all published in 1965) testified to the more traditional values of an older generation. Rahv, Trilling, and Wilson had grown up with the masterpieces of high modernism. In the 1960s, when Eliot and his peers had become institutionalized and even taught on college syllabi, these elder statesmen of letters began to take stock of the modernist revolution. On the one hand, the mythical undercurrents of the great modern classics robbed literature of its purchase on the social and the real; on the other hand, the moderns introduced into literary studies a condescension and even a hostility toward the past. Trilling wittily described the effects of this revolution on his Columbia undergraduates, who thought that "the real subject of all study is the modern world; that the justification of all study is its immediate and presumably practical relevance to modernity; that the true purpose of all study is to lead the young person to be at home in, and in control of, the modern world."[7] America too faced the prospect of fragmenting into two cultures manned on one side by the young, for whom the modern remained the measure of all things, and on the other side by the old, who tried vainly to point to the important achievements of a past the young grew daily less able to recognize.

Kermode's reviewing allowed him to develop his own views on this generational battle. He too noticed the appearance of a new reading public, but his readers, unlike Trilling's, seemed "a little bored" by the elaborate rhetoric of modernist literature (*PE*, 86). Rather than the deferred gratifications of *Finnegans Wake*, they sought the spontaneous combustions of Mailer's *An American Dream*. Or, if the prospect of the visceral appalled them, they sought the slick, state-of-the-art novelty of Salinger's *Franny and Zooey*. In *Puzzles and Epiphanies* (1962), a collection of reviews published between 1958 and 1961, Kermode offered an organized account of these new manifestations. Contemporary literature, he decided, swung between the poles of self-conscious play (the puzzles of Nabokov's *Bend Sinister*, the choreography of Isherwood's *The Memorial* and Powell's *Casanova's Chinese Restaurant*) and the strong apostolic conviction of art as a vehicle for secular revelation that lay behind Durrell's *Alexandria Quartet*, Miller's *The Colossus of Maroussi*, and David Jones's *Epoch and Artist*. Even so, the epiphanies were becoming increasingly puzzling, moving further and further into antinomian privacy. "To every man his own *Vision*, his own answer to Darwin, Huxley, and their successors" (*PE*, 32).

Kermode remained unsatisfied with these developments. He recognized that an art deprived of its metaphysical backdrop would inevitably become arid, at its best a "puzzle." Yet he remained thoroughly skeptical about any modern bid to enforce absolute assent to private epiphanies. During this period, however, Kermode discovered one modern writer who seemed to transcend

35

the usual categories. He found a valuable ally in Wallace Stevens, to whom he devoted a short book in 1960. In Stevens, Kermode saw a poet who was skeptical and even relativist where his contemporaries were dogmatic, and who thought that the imagination could accommodate itself to any time and place, even the most ordinary evenings in New Haven. No wonder then that in *The Sense of an Ending* Kermode wrote of Stevens as the poet who "at this time, speaks more urgently and congenially to me than any other" (*SE*, 156). According to Kermode, Stevens looked on a demythologized universe without resystematizing it according to any occult dogma, willing to let his imagination work in and from it rather than above and beyond it. Kermode saw the meditative operation of the imagination as Stevens's true subject, "what human beings must add to the plain sense of things, in order to make of the world something that suffices."[8] After prolonged immersion in the party of schism and the party of myth, he discovered at last a fellow spokesman for the party of skeptical accommodation.

Kermode found further hints toward this accommodation in his work in the Renaissance. In Edmund Spenser, he discovered a poet convinced that he was writing in the middle of a European spiritual crisis. But Spenser did not seek to explain this crisis by reference to a global myth or by retreating into the past. Instead, he "saw this world as a vast infolded, mutually relevant structure, as inclusive as the Freudian dream; but he also saw it as disconnected, decaying, mutable, disorderly" (*SSD*, 36). In his British Academy Warton lecture *Spenser and the Allegorists* (1962), Kermode contrasted Spenser's double-edged respect for contingency and for pattern with D. H. Lawrence's eagerness to sacrifice everything to pattern. After reviewing the apocalypses of both writers, Kermode decided that Spenser's imagination paid more respect to temporality, adding that his ability "to find in the present moment senses which are enriched, but not absorbed, by the ancient images" might still prove useful. "We need," he concluded, "a better understanding of this sober and confident humanity, of the methods by which Spenser provided contexts in which the archetypes find a present meaning" (*SSD*, 31).

Kermode's most significant work of these years, *The Sense of an Ending*, aims to reconcile the long perspectives of medieval apocalypse he uncovered in Spenser with the existential fortuity of a Stevens or a Sartre. In a world without the certainties of providence, what happens to Spenserian archetypes such as apocalypse, prophecy, and fulfillment? But Kermode has other interests too, some of which seem bewilderingly diverse. How, for example, can he show a common thread behind apocalypses and literary plots? What does Joachim of Flora share with W. B. Yeats? How does the study of Aquinas illuminate Shakespearean tragedy? These are not questions to which every bosom returns an echo, a point that more than one reader en route from Spenser to Sartre was to make in protest.

The contents of his book indicate the remarkable sweep of Kermode's achievement. The relationship between crisis and literary form provides the starting point for a first chapter that moves from Revelation to Robbe-Grillet, taking in Abraham Cowley, Sir Philip Sidney, Joachim of Flora, Austin Farrer, D. H. Lawrence, Henry James, R. G. Collingwood, Dostoevsky, and Albert Camus on the way. The crucial concept of *fiction* discussed in the second chapter takes us through Nietzsche, Hans Vaihinger, C. K. Ogden, I. A. Richards, E. H. Gombrich, and Ortega y Gasset, among others. An investigation of fictions of origin follows next. Kermode's pace slows down to consider Ernst Kantorowicz, Thomas Mann, Aristotle, Aquinas, Spenser, and Shakespeare. In the next chapter, arrival in the modern world entails dialogue with a variety of authorities; Kermode's discrimination among modernisms calls for brief encounters with Yeats, Pound, Wyndham Lewis, Joyce, and Eliot on the one side, and Emmett

Williams, Jack Kerouac, Ken Kesey, and William Burroughs on the other. The last two chapters of the book appear almost meager in the terms that Kermode has set, since they focus almost exclusively on the fictions of absolute deprivation and ultimate need exemplified by Jean-Paul Sartre's *Nausea* and Christopher Burney's *Solitary Confinement*.

Kermode's book originated in the Mary Flexner lectures delivered at Bryn Mawr in 1965. When they appeared two years later as *The Sense of an Ending*, their breadth of interests and novelty of approach drew more attention than their implicit reorientation of postwar critical theory. In the *Listener*, Graham Hough acknowledged that Kermode had produced "a work of great subtlety and considerable importance," but he objected to an "apocalyptic-allusive style" that induced, he thought, "a state of elevated bewilderment." In *Kenyon Review*, Christopher Ricks's article "Fictions and Their Status" presented the book as a source for illuminating readings rather than for coherent categories. "His basic terms," he argued, "don't seem to me to have been as carefully considered as his basic texts."[9] For many of its reviewers, the book served as a quarry for dazzling explications; its broader observations on time, modernity, and fictional form went unnoticed.

Kermode, whose *Romantic Image* tried to restore the sense of time to literary studies, cannot have felt gratified when his next theoretical work was ransacked for readings. The starting point of *The Sense of an Ending* is the antithesis between human needs and temporal contingency. Kermode argues that since reality so conspicuously lacks order and organization, men have devised a variety of "fictions" to "make sense of" the times they occupy on earth. They ask for two things from their fictions. On the one hand, fictions must embody a pattern of "concordance," and thus display in their structure the regularity, system, and unity lacking in the universe as a whole. On the other hand, fictions must honor a complementary deference to contingency, to things as they are in an unshaped actuality. At the two extremes of the fiction-making spectrum are the Bible and the novel. In the Bible, an absolute match between world and word applies. Its opening invokes origins ("In the beginning was the Word"), while its last words look forward to the end ("Even so, come, Lord Jesus"). The correspondence between world and book becomes much more problematic in the novel. From the allegorical opening of *Tom Jones* with Squire Allworthy in Paradise Hall, the novel moves to the mixture of moral essay and chronicle that characterizes *Middlemarch*. In its most recent developments, the novel resists any attempt to schematize its contents. Robbe-Grillet violates the conventions of the detective novel in *The Erasers*; Michel Butor offers a surplus of clues but an absence of meaning in *Passing Time*.

Within these extremes, Kermode scrutinizes a range of fictions, from the scientific (which enable scientists to see light as moving in waves and particles) and legal (where wives are always deemed to have died before husbands in accidents in order to ease the payment of death duties), to the eschatological (in which the expectation of apocalypse, for all its perpetual disconfirmation, continues to shape the behavior of believers in the present). It will be noted that Kermode's scheme does not argue for the superiority or the priority of aesthetic fictions. Instead, he sees aesthetic fictions as working along with other fictions as a necessary mode of understanding a reality that lacks shape and coherence.

Kermode's main interest lies in temporal fictions. He begins by looking at the most simple of these, the *tick-tock* by which time comes to speak the language men use. He sees this kind of fiction as the most modest type of "what we call a plot, an organization that humanizes time by giving it form" (*SE*, 45). Where *tick-tock* registers the contingent duration of time, apocalypse provides a model of its larger pattern. The fiction of apocalypse, Kermode argues, rests in the "human need . . . to humanize the common death" (*SE*, 7). Such fictions account for beginnings and ends; the times between must likewise be given meaning in ways that are true to the human experience of change and wish for permanence. Kermode shows how much of the human attitude to time is projective, a matter of devising fictions to understand "times which are concordant and full" and to fill times that are "mere chronicity" (*SE*, 49–50).

Kermode sees in the fiction a way to accommodate the modern mind's simultaneous rage for and suspicion of order. For this reason, some of the most polemical pages of his book attack the two branches of modernism that have helped to dissociate the modern consciousness by focusing exclusively on one of these. The first, as represented by Wyndham Lewis, T. E. Hulme, and Ezra Pound, places all its bets on the former; the second, as represented by William Burroughs, Jack Kerouac, and Allen Ginsberg, can pledge itself only to the latter. Time is the measure for all fictions, according to Kermode, and to the degree that it takes no account of the claims of past and future, ideal and contingent, a fiction will inevitably fail.

In fact, Kermode argues that in such cases fiction rots into myth. Myths do not belong to time but rather to a golden age beyond time. They offer a form of explanation as total as the fiction is provisional. They call for an absolute form of assent available only in the closed society of rigid hierarchies and minimal expectations that Eliot celebrates in *After Strange Gods*. In the vastly different cultural situation of the mid-1960s, Kermode argues, it is high time that myth was superseded.

Kermode's own theory, he emphasizes, has no connection with utopian mythologies. Its center lies rather in constantly changing human needs. Even the structural features of fictions, like irony in rhetoric or peripeteia in narrative, harmonize with the changing structure of human expectation. Peripeteia, characterized by Kermode as "a disconfirmation followed by a consonance" (*SE*, 18), offers a pattern underpinning both

Christian apocalypse and Shakespearean tragedy. In peripeteia, a structure that simultaneously honors and breaches the pattern of ordinary expectations, Kermode unlocks the dual impulse that underlies the fiction, "a permanent need to live by the pattern" (*SE*, 11) together with "the process of sophisticating the paradigm" (*SE*, 27). Such an antithesis figures most nakedly in the activities of apocalyptic sects, which retain their prophetic patterns even when their predictions have elapsed without fulfillment. In these cases, a disappointed pattern seems preferable to a reality completely without pattern. A more complex accommodation to human needs occurs in scientific research. J. Robert Oppenheimer reports on physicists who harmonize their various views of the universe in "a variety of models . . . [that] stand in a complementary relation to one another."[10] The same progression from the simple to the complex underlies *Hamlet*, where the simple model of a revenge play world that sufficed for Kyd and Tourneur becomes Shakespeare's more complex scrutiny of kinship, kingship, and theatricality.

The fiction's twin allegiances to fact and to form emerge most strongly in Kermode's pages on Sartre's *Nausea*. Here, in a novel written by an author who sees contingency as the only source of human freedom, Kermode finds a most unlikely commitment to form. For Sartre must acknowledge that to represent things realistically he must represent the power of the past. The repeated snatches of the tune "Some of These Days" convey his awareness that "even when . . . nothing is given, still not everything can be new. His hero, his beginning and end, his concords, are not in this sense new; they grow in the shadow of earlier beginnings, ends and concords, earlier heroes" (*SE*, 151–52). Sartre's novel typifies the modern situation where fictions are "deeply distrusted and yet humanly indispensable" (*SE*, 150).

Kermode's range in these pages can induce a kind of vertigo in an unsuspecting reader. Not many books reach from A.D. 1000 to the second world war, from Aristotle's *De Anima* to quantum physics, and it is a fair bet to suggest that of those that do still fewer are "studies in the theory of fiction." But as far as Kermode soars, his inquiries are buttressed by three key terms: need; fictions; sense; the human *need* to make *sense* through *fictions*.

Kermode's analysis of human need derives from the work of E. H. Gombrich and I. A. Richards. Both writers show a special concern with the audience's share in artistic representation. In his *Poetries and Sciences* (1926; 1935; 1970), Richards argued that a world severed of mythology and magic would transform the transmission and the reception of artistic experience. Modern art, he thought,

> will be the outgrowth of needs, impulses, attitudes, which did not arise in the same form for poets in the past. And correspondingly—though this we are less willing to acknowledge—the poetry of the past will be read by such a reader in new ways. "The eye altering alters all." A poem no more than any other object is independent of the interests by which it is apprehended. Our attitudes to man, to nature, and to the universe which contains them both change with every generation, and have changed more extensively and more deeply in recent years. . . . When attitudes are changing neither criticism nor poetry remains stationary.[11]

Richards acknowledged that modern poetry could not remain independent of its readers. As a teacher, he frequently attacked the clichéd conceptions his students brought to bear, encouraging instead a more complex approach to the experience of reading.

Gombrich's famous words, "The innocent eye sees nothing," reflect a similar concern with the interested perceptions that observers bring to bear. However, Gombrich, unlike Richards, has always recognized that a sophisticated eye may see too much and that observers trained in complexity might project their own perceptions onto the works they examine. Accordingly,

Gombrich has developed the idea of "making sense" to stabilize this process, to make sure that the complexity of interests taken to the artwork does not dictate the interpretation of it. Gombrich draws a clear line between artist and interpreter, arguing,

> Whenever an ancient cult image, the pattern on a brooch, a broken column or a painted potsherd ask to be interpreted, any historian worth his salt will try to make sense of it in such terms as his creative imagination suggests. But a critical mind will not rest content with this vision. He will watch for further evidence to fit it into the image of the lost culture. Usually, of course, such further evidence is available in one form or another, and the historian's task is precisely to fit it all together into a context that "makes sense."[12]

The historian's "making sense" results from a contractual alliance between convention and perception, past and present. It is a reconstitutive act, one that knits the object as it exists in the imagination to the imagination as it exists in a context of similar objects. To understand the way that artworks exist in relation to other artworks falls to the historian, the custodian of tradition. Gombrich sees tradition as the "undistorted memories" of conventions, contexts, and situations that historians have slowly rebuilt by fitting works of art "into a context that 'makes sense.'"

In Gombrich's scheme of things, sense-making respects the boundaries between past and present, absence and presence. But when Kermode chooses the fiction as his instrument of sense-making, he blurs Gombrich's clear distinction. In so far as fictions are ubiquitous in the modern world, one cannot dispute his need to invoke them. Yet the specific sources from which he derives the term point to the problems in which it will involve him. The principal source, of course, is the Stevens who stated, "Poetry is the supreme fiction." But Stevens also acknowledged other fictions, and pointed to a common playfulness in them all: "fictive things / Wink as they will. Wink most when widows wince." The poet's supremacy, he suggests, arises from his ability to repopulate the vacancy of reality. He contrasts the "brilliant pages" of poetry with "the barren reality" of an ordinary landscape, with its "sense of abandonment and destitution, the sense that, after all, the vast mausoleum of human memory is emptier than one had supposed."[13] In Stevens's eyes, the fiction plays artificially across a reality that runs naturally to decline.

Hans Vaihinger's *The Philosophy of "As If"* (1924), which Kermode also cites in the course of his book, does not confine itself to aesthetic fictions. Vaihinger includes among these ways of "finding our way about the world" legal, psychological, scientific, and administrative fictions. Logical fictions supply men with categories by which to organize the world, while causal fictions help to make it cohere. But behind all fictions, aesthetic and nonaesthetic, stands the impulse to imagine an alternative to contingent reality. Indeed, Vaihinger, who described humanity as "a species of monkey suffering from megalomania," did not harbor too many benevolent illusions about either human beings or reality. For Vaihinger as for Stevens, reality is random, unorganized, and literally unimaginable. In a long appendix, Vaihinger acknowledges the inspiration of Nietzsche in the construction of his theory. In these pages, the subversive and nihilistic potential of the fiction becomes prominent as Nietzsche describes his aim of standing Plato on his head. "'My philosophy is an inverted Platonism: the further it is from actual reality, the purer, more beautiful and better it becomes.'"[14] For all these writers, the fiction's power to delight increases in direct proportion to its distance from reality. Whether its primary context be scientific or behavioral, its governing impulse remains aesthetic.

It is clear that two radically opposite views of reality and two distinct modes of perception underlie the terms Kermode sets at the foundation of his discussion. Gombrich devised the idea of making sense to ballast the opportunities for unrestricted liberty involved in making *need* the basis of critical reconstructions. But by borrowing the idea of fictions from Stevens, Nietzsche, and Vaihinger, Kermode disturbs the balance again, for the fictions these authors describe invariably become more creative than reconstructive. Behind Gombrich's idea of making sense lies the assumption of an ordered reality. "Chaos . . . is in itself a human creation. Whatever the world of an amoeba or an earthworm may be like, it is certainly not chaotic but structured. Where there is life there is order."[15] In consequence, the gap between imagination and reality or perceiver and object never exceeds the human capacity to reconstruct it. But it is exactly this gap across which the fiction-maker constructs his fictions. According to Vaihinger, the fiction does not rest "content with the material given" but rather "can adapt foreign elements to its own requirements as easily as it adapts itself to what is new."[16] For Vaihinger, Stevens, and Nietzsche, illumination comes from the creative imperative to construct something out of nothing.

Kermode's book derives its power from its desire to bring different areas of knowledge together. Yet it is not easy to see how he can accommodate the discrepancy between his instrument, the fiction, and his purpose, making sense. How can the fiction, a re-creative or regulative instrument, be harnessed to sense-making, a reconstitutive act? Is the sense we make through a fiction something we project onto the world or something we discover in it? Unlike Kermode, Gombrich draws a firm line between projection and re-creation. He acknowledges that artistic representation may originate in the former, but he insists that the art historian subordinate projection to intention. "We must try to relearn the difference between stimulation through self-projection, which, when applied to art, so often passes for 'appreciation,' and that enrichment that comes from an understanding, however dim and imperfect, of what a great work of art is *intended* to convey."[17] But when he sets the fiction at the center of his discussion, Kermode collapses Gombrich's firm distinction between critic and artist. In the same year that he published *The Sense of an Ending*, he told readers of the *New York Review of Books*, "The one obvious thing about *Hamlet* is that nobody could possibly say what it *means*." Where intentions and meanings become unfathomable, only one conclusion can immediately be drawn: "Criticism is now most certainly an art."[18] In Kermode's scheme all things become fictions, from the modest structures a critic erects to understand a work of art and abandons as soon as he has secured some illumination, to the poet's ambitious aim to enclose "reality and justice" in a single visionary system. Kermode collapses reality into a set of interlocking projections, as his discussion of Yeats's *A Vision* makes clear. "The System is a plot, a purely human projection, though not more human than its apparent antithesis, reality, which is a human imagining of the inhuman" (*SE*, 105). By paring down *human* until it means *fiction-creating*, Kermode reaches a point where reality stands only for a void to be filled by fictions.

But the drift of his argument cuts away the ground on which Kermode stands. He began his book by arguing for the power of precedent, "especially at a moment in history when it may be harder than ever to accept the precedents of sense-making—to believe that any earlier way of satisfying one's need to know the shape of life in relation to the perspectives of time will suffice" (*SE*, 3). As he continues, however, Kermode concedes more and more to the exigencies of the contemporary. A similar drift occurs in his style, where a chameleon *we* yields increasingly to the topic it happens to discuss. When it treats of Aquinas it is Aquinan. When it attacks the aberrations of the modern it sounds like Gombrich. When it speaks of prisons, its tone becomes sepulchral. The fiction is a device too constricted to a particular situation or problem to serve as an ordering principle for a book, least of all a book that aims to make sense of the way we order our whole lives. The anarchic tendencies of the fiction undercut the constructive needs of extended critical prose.

The third element in Kermode's triad, *need*, can do nothing to resolve the conflicting demands of *fiction* and *sense-making*. For Kermode makes no systematic attempt to calibrate the variety of human needs, political and social as well as psychological and metaphysical. His analysis of apocalypse as a radical fiction overlooks the way activists from Jan of Leyden to Karl Marx have used the notion of apocalypse to reshape the political future. Nor does he engage systematically with the changing function of apocalypse in different historical periods. For instance, his "drastic foreshortenings" admit only the slightest of references to temporal fictions in the realistic novel or the historical narrative, even though both have provided essential instruments to make sense of lives in a secular age. His argument shifts from the simple to the complex, from the sacred to the existential without considering any middle ground.

Nor, despite his interest in the insights of intellectual history, does Kermode employ the usual tools of the historian of ideas, a discipline that owes its development to Arthur O. Lovejoy, who saw the subject as a way to break down the barriers that specialization had erected in the universities. Lovejoy's bias was always philosophical, his method rigorously analytical, his interest in ideas rather than in texts per se. Such a procedure can endanger the imaginative life of the works it encounters. Historians of ideas have always been fond of Neoplatonism, and some less subtle practitioners have discovered it serendipitously everywhere from *Jack Juggler* and *Perkin Warbeck* to *Paradise Lost*. In the 1950s and the 1960s, writers like Lionel Trilling, Richard Hoftstader, and Jacques Barzun, who all appeared alongside Kermode in *Encounter* and *Partisan Review*, tried to divert the history of ideas to a less austerely philosophical context. These writers emphasized how ideas functioned as political weapons or as slogans for rival factions. To understand the history of an idea it seemed necessary to understand its use in a specific time and situation. In recent years, J. G. A. Pocock and Quentin Skinner have carried this contextualization even further by arguing that the historian of ideas must reconstruct the specific illocutionary framework of an idea before he can claim to understand its history.

Kermode's own contribution toward this redefinition amounts to an existential history of ideas. He wants to understand how inherited ideas and images impinge on consciousness by clinging to the minds of those who entertain them. He is therefore less eager to analyze the various elements of his more important ideas than to re-create from within their affective force. Unlike Lovejoy, Kermode will not map out some sixty shades of meaning clustering around the word *nature*. And unlike Raymond Williams in *Culture and Society* or William Empson in *The Structure of Complex Words*, he does not set key words in the light of specific careers and texts. He tends rather to choose ideas like *crisis* that are more susceptible to association than to analysis. Kermode proceeds by meditation around an idea rather than by systematic investigation of its contexts.

But without these nets to play his observations against, Kermode comes to sound like a latter-day Victorian sage. Like the sage, he finds his topic in the ache of modernity as perceived under the enormous vistas of time. His inquiry, like the sage's, derives from impulses more metaphysical than scholarly and critical. His drastic foreshortenings and arresting analogies serve not so much a central argument as a central belief: out of our multiplicity of fictions we will arrive at "something *real*" (*SE*, 18). Kermode, it will be noted, speaks on *our* behalf; that too is the prerogative of the sage. Indeed, he avails himself of several such prerogatives. His "something *real*" recalls Matthew Arnold's habit of offering emphases for explanations, while his description of apocalyptic fictions as originating in "the human need . . . to humanize the common death" bestrides the centuries with a confident authority that one key, like Carlyle's life force or Arnold's spirit of criticism, will unlock them all.

If *The Sense of an Ending* adopts the rhetoric of the Victorian sage, it also retains his serious purposes. It aims to move across the battle lines of the postwar age of polarization and to get its various factions talking again. If *Romantic Image* modestly aimed at revising the categories of literary theory, then *The Sense of an Ending* moves more boldly across the lines of intellectual, cultural, and sacred history. How far the book succeeds in its own ambitious aims is obviously another matter. Kermode's refusal to allow literature to dictate the terms of cultural debate marks a move forward from *Romantic Image*, where a literary movement determined the shape of cultural history. In *The Sense of an Ending*, literature takes its place alongside other instruments that human beings have developed to understand the shape of their experiences in time. What becomes less certain is Kermode's conviction about the permanence of the patterns of which men avail themselves to understand their world. Kermode becomes so obsessed by the obsolescence of these patterns, so convinced that they reflect only the interests of their users ("It is ourselves we encounter whenever we invent fictions" [*SE*, 38–39]), that his book becomes progressively less convincing about the possibility of any continuities in culture or any movement outside self-reflexiveness.

The book takes on a peculiarly schizoid quality as it continues. A conciliatory account of the complementary relationship between past paradigms and present conditions fades into a puzzled elegy on the intractability of a present that reflects only its own image. And although it shows very strongly the influence of E. H. Gombrich, the book has none of Gombrich's confidence in the transmissibility of artistic conventions. Kermode and Gombrich both look hard at the intellectual historian's *topos* of the relationship between permanence and change. But Kermode's convictions rest on the ubiquity of change while Gombrich pledges his learning to the virtues of permanence. By committing himself to the fiction as the instrument by which the individual makes what sense he can of the world, Kermode makes his forms volitional rather than institutional. And in the process, he submits himself to the very myth of the solitary artist and void-like universe that Gombrich had hoped to eradicate by his idea of making sense. By the end of his book, Kermode has changed the symbolist myth of a once-and-for-all catastrophe for an existentialist myth of an ongoing daily crisis.

IV. THE CLASSIC

IN the last pages of *The Sense of an Ending*, Kermode emphasized the terrible liberty of the modern world. "In our perpetual crisis," he commented, "we have, at the proper seasons, under the pressure perhaps of our own end, dizzying perspectives upon the past and the future, in a freedom which is the freedom of a discordant reality" (*SE*, 179). In the middle of a crisis that subjected reality to change at an unprecedented rate, Kermode turned his attention to that monument to continuity, the classic. Unlike the fiction, by definition provisional and disposable, the classic has lasted. Cultures look to their classics to transmit larger values rather than to solve particular problems; the classic's strength is paradigmatic rather than operational. Even so, the classic does not form a separate enclave in Kermode's criticism. From 1963, when he first wrote on the subject, he has ambitiously aimed at understanding our perpetual crises and our cultural monuments simultaneously.

Kermode began to consider the classic in a review-essay entitled "Survival of the Classics" (*Encounter*, 1963). At this point he stressed the dangers the classic faced from a criticism too exclusive in its canon formation or too arid in its procedures. Could the classic survive the rigorism of a Winters or the pedantry of the graduate schools? Following this essay, Kermode began a six-year investigation into Shakespeare's status as a classic. In a series of reviews published in the *New York Review of Books* between 1964 and 1969, he considered whether scholars and avant-garde directors had modified Shakespeare's classic status. Much of his inquiry centered on *King Lear*, a play then subject to the restless innovations of director's theater. Did such innovations endanger the classic as an object or did they prolong its survival? After seven years of thought, Kermode's answer arrived in "Survival of the Classic" (published 1971), a lecture best described as an exercise in historical phenomenology. Kermode accepted the principle that the classic could only survive as a valued object in the minds of readers able to reconstruct it according to lights that their own culture would find valid. He then showed how *King Lear* had proved equal to the demands of critics as different as Samuel Johnson, George Orwell, and, in 1970, Frank Kermode.

Characteristically, Kermode's approach to the topic now broadened. In the 1970s, he began to move away from Shakespeare and to consider the question of the classic more theoretically. In 1973, he delivered the T. S. Eliot Memorial lectures at the University of Kent. In 1975, he published these in book form as *The Classic*. With Kermode's customary breadth, the lectures move from Virgil to Dante, from Milton to Marvell, from Addison to Dilthey. The last chapters of the book, like *The Sense of an Ending*, examine two typically unexpected modern instances, in this case Nathaniel Hawthorne and Emily Brontë. At this point, Kermode's inquiry into the classic and his inquiry into modernity come together in ways that were to prove exceedingly controversial.

Even as late as 1985, classics remained on Kermode's mind. In *Forms of Attention*, seeking to understand "by what means . . . we attribute value to works of art," he uses those indisputable classics Botticelli and Shakespeare as case studies for his inquiry.[1] For almost twenty years, then, Kermode has sought to understand the kinds of art that become classics, the extent to which their survival can be guaranteed, and the means by which their values may be transmitted.

In considering the classic, Kermode has of course taken up a stock question for literary discussion. Among the illustrious names who preceded him in asking, "What is a classic?," Johnson, Sainte-Beuve, Arnold, and Eliot spring immediately to mind. And, interestingly, these writers share a broad unanimity in their answers. Each of them sees age and continued esteem as the first criterion for classic status. Horace sets down a hundred years as the minimum for admission. Sainte-Beuve, who considers the nature of the classic "a delicate question," concedes that a classic is "an author of past times, already hallowed by general admiration, who is an authority in his own style." Johnson's famous *Preface* of 1765 announces that because Shakespeare "has long outlived his century, the term commonly fixed as the test of literary merit," he can now "begin to assume the dignity of an ancient." Johnson's discussion rests on a belief he shares with other famous writers on this topic, in an unbroken line of continuity that links past to present. These temporal continuities, Johnson submits, allow a later age to benefit from the perpetually springing wisdom of its predecessors. "What mankind have long possessed they have often examined and compared, and if they persist to value the possession, it is because frequent comparisons have confirmed opinion in its favour."[2]

Time confers value on the classic; but in the same way, Eliot argues, the classic can confer value on time as an embodiment of civilized aspirations and attachments. In Eliot, the classic becomes cosmopolitan rather than commonplace. He describes an *Aeneid* with a hero who is not so much Aeneas as the destiny Aeneas moves toward, the fulfillment of European civilization itself: "behind the story of Aeneas is the consciousness of a more radical distinction, a distinction which is at the same time a statement of *relatedness*, between two great cultures, and, finally, of their reconciliation under an all-embracing destiny."[3] Both Johnson and Eliot see a progressively unfolding universal and providential order as guaranteeing the survival of the classic and enabling it to persist in its exemplary capacity. Sainte-Beuve's definition neatly combines the ethical convictions of Johnson with the cosmopolitan aspirations of Eliot. "A true classic, as I should like to hear it defined, is an author who has enriched the human mind, who has really augmented its treasures, who has made it take one more step forward, who has discovered some unequivocal moral truth."[4] Some such belief in a stock of moral and civic certitudes underlies the answer of all these authorities to the question, "What is a classic?"

Almost inevitably, therefore, discussions of the classic press toward the public domain. Johnson, for example, sees in Shakespeare's works "a system of civil and oeconomical prudence."[5] Eliot thinks that the authority of the *Aeneid* "is due to the unique position in our history of the Roman Empire and the Latin language."[6] Even the skeptical Sainte-Beuve hints that the survival of many classics has called for considerable institutional sleight of hand. He points to the case of Homer, to whom, he notes, "it has been necessary to attribute . . . a design, a plan, literary intentions, qualities of criticism and urbanity as an afterthought of which he would certainly never have dreamt."[7] Such interpretative accommodations demonstrate that classics sound much alike in critical commentary, however much they differ at the time of reading. Sainte-Beuve testifies to the unanimity among interpreters of the classic, who repeatedly find in their chosen texts a treasure house of order, urbanity, and design.

But how can the classic, for generations the epitome of conformity, survive in a time of crisis and dissent? Kermode undertakes to investigate the classic at a time when the very temporal and institutional agencies entrusted with its survival are themselves the subject of debate. He cannot rely on any informed consensus about the inevitability of progress or providence; neither Johnson's common sense nor Eliot's privileged destiny underprops his inquiries. How can he make the classic speak to an age of crisis?

Time and the academy, for his predecessors the guardians of the classic, become for Kermode the greatest threats to its present survival. In his review-essay "Survival of the Classics," he describes two waves of critical assault that the twentieth century has directed at the classic. The critical revolution inaugurated by Eliot,

Leavis, and Winters questioned established reputations such as Spenser and Milton and for a time succeeded in driving both from the canon. By the 1960s, however, both authors regained some critical favor. Even so, Kermode remained worried by the conditions of their restoration, for their commentators did not restore them in terms of the living continuities on which the classic had customarily depended. Instead they employed the arcane lore of the graduate school, where in order to reconstruct what seemed "a self-evident truth to eighteenth-century commentators" modern critics entered a different dimension, a universe "to be recovered, like the sense of Spenser's dream-world." In a related essay of this period, "Marvell Transprosed," Kermode deplored the lack of an "inwardness with the historical processes" that the graduate schools exhibited, and he called for a kind of interpretation that would once again exhibit the power of the classic to live inside the consciousness of the thoughtful reader.[8]

Two attempts made by important literary critics to achieve this inwardness cannot have escaped Kermode's attention. In 1963, Roland Barthes's *On Racine* made a bid to rescue the classic French poet from his commentators. Barthes severed literary study into two autonomous realms, "one historical, to the degree that literature is an institution; the other psychological, to the degree that it is creation."[9] This critic preferred to focus on Racine's imaginative world rather than his working environment and, instead of attempting to recover his intentions and influences, took a reconstitutive and even playful approach, trying on his author a series of self-conscious modern schemata. Ten years later, Harold Bloom's *The Anxiety of Influence* (1973) sketched the program for a revisionary literary history that would reverse the Anglo-American modernist canon. Kermode, who saw Eliot's revised critical canon as exclusive and anti-historical, could only have been interested in Bloom's project. Even so, he may have found it disappointing, for Bloom's Judaic, Darwinist, and romanticist manifesto looked more like a reverse shot of the Anglo-Catholic, royalist, and classicist program that Eliot unfurled in *For Lancelot Andrewes* (1928) than a genuine reconstruction of literary history. Bloom renovated tradition by supplying it with its latest shot of catastrophe theory, although this time the catastrophe took place inside the minds of the English poets rather than in the mind of England as a whole. In short, Bloom derived his account of the relationship between tradition and the individual talent from Eliot only to annihilate Eliot.

For Kermode, such radical maneuvering must have induced mixed feelings. Enough of a historian to respect continuity, he remained enough of a skeptic to mistrust complete change. Barthes's belief in the reader's role in reconstructing the classic supported the tendency of Kermode's own work, but his polarization of literary study into two realms merely repeated, with local variations, the anti-historicism of the New Critics. Bloom, on the other hand, simply stood Eliot on his head. Kermode himself proceeded more cautiously than either. From 1967 to 1974, he chaired a series of informal seminars on influential modern masters at University College, London, that included Levi-Strauss, Lacan, and Foucault. Some of these critics later appeared in the *Modern Masters* series for which Kermode served as general editor and to which in 1973 he himself contributed a volume on D. H. Lawrence. During the same period, he extended his acquaintanceship with the counterculture in a series of talks for BBC radio called "Political Metaphors" and "Is an Elite Necessary?" in which he reflected on the radicalization of institutions such as the family and the arts. In *The Sense of an Ending*, Kermode seemed more eager to condemn the new culture than to make sense of it. Now, with 1968, the year of revolutions, only just behind him, he realized that the larger continuities of humanist culture depended on some sort of mediation with the new. These talks took him far from the usual academic networks. He interviewed, among others, pop music manager Joe Boyd, television dramatist John Hopkins, comic scriptwriter Johnny Speight, rock journalist Mick Farren, and Stuart Brisley, whose speciality was staging performance art in Edinburgh car showrooms.

Closer familiarity with the new culture allowed Kermode to consider the possibility of accommodation. Moreover, he was willing to concede its identity as a significantly new phenomenon. In an uncanny echo of Eliot's famous comment in "The Metaphysical Poets," Kermode told listeners that "something has happened" to a society that seriously asks itself the question, "Are hierarchies necessary?" During the same period, he told his fellow humanists in *Partisan Review* that unlike Eliot he would not follow a backward pointing path. The recent campus upheavals reminded academics that "we should not be so absurd as to teach as if there were powerful forces not ourselves that more or less oblige aspiring human beings to be like us. . . . Other social universes have their own reality constructions." In 1967, Kermode reminded the neo-modernists that every new communication must have some relation to the past. In 1970, he reminded fellow humanists that all tradition needed some significant relation to the new, if its survival were to be guaranteed. "We have changed, and must change again," he warned them. The need now was to explore "new ways of making the monuments new, taking them out of the temporal rat race, changing them as needed."[10]

From 1963 to 1970, Kermode chose his own monument and was busily making it new. His monument was Shakespeare, whom he had to salvage from the attentions of the counterculture and the academy alike. While both these groups concurred in assigning to the Bard only the simplest of intentions, Kermode emphasized his complexity. "Nowhere did Shakespeare do more to disconcert his audience," he observed of *Hamlet*. "One can, certainly, see a man dull enough to see only what matched his commonplace expectations, but who wants to know him?" By burying the text under a rubble of information, scholarship only interred the classic. "The play itself doubts, delays, acts, is cautious and mad, sweeps to and abstains from revenge, prevaricates and speaks true. The minute you forget that the play does all these things, and begin instead to speak of a necessary conformity—in the play, and in *all* its audiences—to Christian precept, or to the audience's ethical set, you are talking about something else, not about this unique work."[11] By emphasizing the unique and the nonconforming, Kermode implicitly offered a significantly different account of classical properties. If authors from Johnson to Eliot saw in the classic the perfection of the common, Kermode's characterization, which emphasized the puzzling illumination of the unique, made a bid to preserve the classic for an age dedicated to the erosion of classical authority.

If he met scholarly conservatism with interpretative ingenuity, Kermode countered directorial novelty with scholarly caution. In 1964, he found Peter Brook's production of *King Lear* less than fully satisfying, with Paul Scofield's Lear displaying "the loss of some of the great basic rhythms of the piece."[12] While acknowledging the production's power, Kermode deplored the way "a traditionless theatre" depended on inspired invention. He insisted on the authority of Shakespeare's own words, objecting to cuts and to gratuitous substitutions that enforced a directorial meaning on Shakespeare's text.

Kermode reached the climax of his dual inquiry into the nature of the classic and its relations with the modern in his lecture "Survival of the Classic" (published in 1971). The lecture moves from a review of a variety of critical responses to *King Lear* to Kermode's own attempt to reconstruct the play for the moderns, before concluding with a definition of the classic as a text that accommodates itself to the paradigms its audiences bring to it. Kermode takes up Orwell's challenge to "'shut your eyes and think of *King Lear*,'" a process designed to discover "'the bare skeleton of the play'" (*SSD*, 167). Kermode notes with interest that his own skeleton is not

Orwell's any more than Orwell's was Tolstoy's or Johnson's. Yet the play can absorb all these rival speculations, leaving any critic with "a sense that there was too much of it for one's perception, or anybody else's, to organize, so that the work seems, if not a chaos, at least a system of potentialities beyond one's power to actualize them" (*SSD*, 175).

This view of the classic as a text with a meaning in excess of its reader's organizing power differs markedly from the traditional view of the classic as arbiter and authority. Kermode replaces the imperialistic vocabulary of Eliot or Sainte-Beuve with his own quizzical imagery.

> One could say that a classic, surviving, will have in some measure an obsessed, dreamlike quality, which nevertheless does not resist sharp and simple demands for significance. My belief is that Shakespeare, at his most powerful, supplies just this kind of thing, having devised public expressions for the deepest and most obsessed of his meanings. . . . It might be said, for example, that he was more than usually interested in vicious sexuality and madness. Long before we get down to the displaced archetypes, we have to contend with this extraordinary, reticent, obsessed person, who was in a world of dream, vision, madness, and yet talked sense, sense that satisfies the undemanding whose franchise counts for the classic, nearly all the time. (*SSD*, 178–79)

His *Lear* is "obsessed," "multiple," "a chaos." Where it is not "reticent" it misleads; "what is given with one voice is taken away with another" (*SSD*, 169–79). The result is a romantic version of the classic that releases it for a world without final authorities or determinate structure. Kermode also provides the classic with a significantly different kind of reader. In choosing to read the play with the intensity extended to a dream and the attentiveness afforded to a legal document, he acts as a representative post-romantic reader who approaches his classic not so much as a quarry for generalizations as a source for secular revelation. For Kermode, the Shakespearean classic presents an opaque window on an open-ended world.

When he turns from his own skeleton of the play to the critical responses to it, Kermode uncovers the same typically modern set of ambiguous moral touchstones and fragmented world pictures. In Lear's encounter with Gloucester at Dover; in the short scene in which Gloucester learns patience only to be swept further into the flux of events; and in Lear's last words to the dead Cordelia, Kermode finds the "continuity of topic" that ensures the play's survival. He shows that each of these scenes presents a different kind of crisis, either across the generations or across class lines. In the first, a mad king addresses a blind nobleman. In the second, a disguised son lectures a disordered father on the value of activity. In the third, a father laments the loss of his daughter in circumstances that Johnson of all critics has summed up best. Kermode concurs with the view that the ending of the play runs "'contrary to the natural ideas of justice, to the hope of the reader, and what is yet more strange, to the faith of the chronicles'" (*SSD*, 170–71). For Kermode, the preeminence of the classic lies not in the relatedness between different orders of culture that Eliot identified in the *Aeneid* but in the large disruptions it reveals between families, monarchs, and even nature itself. In a way that exactly matches the modern temper, *King Lear* throws out large questions only to annihilate them in its subsequent action. In Kermode's discussion the play's status as wisdom literature (traditionally an important aspect of the classic) matters less than the urgency of its situations. What this central classical text shows us is the imminence of crisis, as character after character watches his pondered formulations and cherished loyalties destroyed by events.

It is easy to see why Kermode considered *King Lear* on five separate occasions between 1964 and 1974. For with its continuous crises, generational disruptions, and resistance to generalization, the play becomes for Kermode the very paradigm of the modern classic. Moreover, his discussion clears the way for a pragmatic view of the classic more suited to modern needs than the objective classic offered by his predecessors. Kermode's classic is a noumenon rather than a phenomenon. Its longevity depends on the attention of a reader, whose role in Kermode's scheme becomes a crucial one. For the reader alone can make the classic new by bringing it into a lively relationship with contemporary reality. Having reached the point where he defines the classic as a text open to readerly reinterpretation, Kermode can now undertake the formidable task of reconciling his own classic with the very different texts described by his eminent predecessors.

*   *   *

What does Kermode's *The Classic* (1975) contribute to this oldest of debates? In brief, Kermode holds on to the methods of his predecessors while relinquishing their assumptions. Like them, he proceeds by comparisons that stretch across centuries and civilizations. Like them, he is truly cosmopolitan, as at home in Rome as in London. Unlike them, his position is finally relativist, since he argues that there is no paradigmatic classic, only classics; no classical values, only values that generations of readers match against the inherent plurality of classic texts.

Kermode continues to see the reader as the chief agency of the classic's survival. In his first chapter, he shows how Eliot's exemplary classic, *The Aeneid*, owed its survival to the activities of two powerful sets of readers, the Roman empire and the Roman Catholic church. His second chapter traces the survival of the classic outside imperial sponsorship. He shows how classical values underwent witty satiric transformations at the hands of Marvell, fervent denials by Milton, and scholarly excavations in the Augustan antiquarianism of Addison. But when the classic becomes a period piece, as it did for the Augustans, Kermode questions whether it still speaks with a living voice to the readers who study it. With the decline of imperial and transcendental sanctions, the classic relies increasingly on exegetical ingenuity and scholarly reconstruction.

But from his third chapter, Kermode takes a new kind of approach to a new kind of classic. When he comes to consider nineteenth- and twentieth-century classics he arms himself with the equipment of the interpreter, the paradigmatic modern reader who can be relied on to produce something new from the texts he encounters. Nathaniel Hawthorne's *The House of the Seven Gables*, with its declining dynasties and uncertain typologies, Kermode sees as the very opposite of Virgil's imperial classic. With the idea of the classic reduced to its lowest terms—standing for any book that is read a long time after it is written—Kermode devotes most of his last chapter to a reading of *Wuthering Heights*. As the occasion demands, he produces the "something new" that in a pluralistic and crisis-ridden society has become the chief requirement for interpretative activity.

Kermode delivered the lectures that form the basis of his *The Classic* in 1973. It is tempting to think that they belong to the aftermath of the 1960s upheavals. The subject is, after all, a traditional one for literary critics, especially eminent ones, since it allows its speaker to borrow from the authority of precedent and to reflect on a suitably broad topic in comfortably general tones. Kermode was soon to be appointed to the King Edward VII Professorship, the senior chair in English at Cambridge. Would his T. S. Eliot Memorial lectures demonstrate his reconciliation with orthodoxy? In title, the occasion promised none of the impulse to revise historical categories that fueled *Romantic Image*. And if the lectures had the range of *The Sense of an Ending*, they moved with a steadier chronological development and with more display of scholarship, risking few of the *concordia discors* that erupted in the earlier book.

Yet *The Classic* has far more explosive consequences for literary history than its predecessors. However placatorily Kermode might speak of reconciling Eliot's views on the classic with his own, *The Classic*, like *Romantic Image*, attacks the premises of Eliot's discussion. For while Eliot contends that "a classic can only occur when a civilization is mature,"[13] Kermode argues that this formulation applies to only one kind of classic. And like *The Sense of an Ending*, *The Classic* shifts in emphasis in the course of its discussion. Kermode begins by paying his respects to continuity; he ends by welcoming "the new Mercury"[14] whose signature is plurality and change.

But even from his first lecture a modification in Kermode's position becomes apparent. He no longer pays any more than perfunctory attention to the classic as an object of value, but he analyzes exceptionally closely the institutions that have bestowed value on it. When he discusses Eliot's "What is a Classic?" he therefore seeks to unpack what he calls the "imperialist" assumptions behind that essay, the conviction that Virgil epitomizes the continuity of European culture and the centrality of the Latin language. Kermode makes his own position clear enough. Unlike the author in whose honor he speaks, he sees "imperialism" as a discredited fiction. Accordingly, he argues, "What we have finally to consider is whether in 'What is a Classic?' Eliot was answering the kind of question we ask a generation later, and whether his answers mean anything to us" (C, 42). Kermode's position is disturbingly forthright; he speaks as if Eliot were as antique as Virgil himself. How, he asks, can one "validate the classic" without recourse to Eliot's "metaphysical or mythical thinking about language and history. . . . How, without mythologizing, are we to explain that the classic retains its identity without refusing to subject itself to change, without losing itself in an abysm of unintelligibility and irrelevance?" (C, 45). Kermode ruthlessly subjects the classic to his own skeptical interrogations. What happens to a classic cut off from its traditional sources of authority? How central is the notion of universality to the classic? How many veils can the classic peel off and still retain its identity? Why have the words of the classic always been less important than the interests it has served?

In the following lectures Kermode moves to consider how the classic survives outside imperial sponsorship. For Milton, who rejected emperors and pagans alike, the classic simply failed to make the transition. Spenser accommodated it to his nationalist propaganda, while Marvell retained it as an ideal pattern against which to measure modern contingencies. After Marvell, Kermode argues, the classic becomes the preserve of the philologists and archaeologists. It is at this time, when the voice of the original becomes unprecedentedly faint, that the quest for the classic authors' intentions and frames of reference begins. The infirmity of the authors signals the appearance of the scholars. Against this background, Kermode's concession that "the books we call classics possess intrinsic qualities that endure" (C, 44) strikes a strangely muted note.

At this point, if the classic is to retain any authority or even any interest, Kermode must find a new technique to approach it. He finds this technique by quoting E. D. Hirsch's description of the liberty of interpretation open to readers of legal texts, which, Hirsch points out, are "'meant to apply to objects and situations which did not exist when the law was formulated and which thus could not be comprehended or comprehensible within that original linguistic domain'" (C, 78). Kermode hints that Hirsch's words might well apply to literary texts too, so it is no surprise to find him, twenty pages later, applying them to the classic. Even so, the analogy is a troubling one, for in moving from classics to literary texts to legal texts Kermode slides down a scale of value. Classics are dense with significance and expressive meaning; literary texts are potentially so; but legal texts carry little in the way of either. The American Declaration of Independence, an evocative enough document in its own right, does not invite the range of interpretations of a classic like *King Lear*. Kermode argues that classics and legal documents alike are "exempted from the temporal restrictions that apply to other texts" (*C*, 78), an analogy that conveniently glosses over the very different ways in which classics and legal documents are read.

At this point in the argument *classic* and *text* become interchangeable. Kermode slips back and forth between them as if in modern times at least the distinction had less and less force. At this stage, the classic loses its last shred of authority and becomes simply "a book that is read a long time after it was written" (*C*, 117). As if to underline the breadth of the definition, Kermode chooses as one of his paradigmatic modern classics *The House of the Seven Gables*, a book that hardly lays claim to any high authority. Instead of the imperial line of Aeneas, Kermode shows us the broken line of Hawthorne's Pyncheons. Instead of the inspired voice of the epic poet, we listen to Hawthorne's evasive and skeptical narration. Instead of the Roman empire with its mission "parcere subjectis et debellare superbos," we are set adrift in a New England where, as Hawthorne's narrator himself confesses, "an infinite, inscrutable blackness has annihilated sight."[15]

In "Survival of the Classic," Kermode presented a kind of romantic classic. In the last chapters of *The Classic*, he gives us the solipsist's classic, a text entirely dependent on the skilled reader's reconstructions. At this point in the argument the reader steps forward as the sole preserver of the classic's life, his means an almost heroic act of interpretation that makes it new with every reading. And not surprisingly, Kermode chooses to close his book not with a simple recapitulation of his premises but with a charismatic demonstration of them. The demonstration focuses on *Wuthering Heights*, a book notable for the isolation of its setting and the puzzling discontinuities of its theme. In keeping with his new emphasis, Kermode approaches the book as a bricolage, not as a monument. He makes no effort to establish a skeleton of the text in his consciousness as he did with

King Lear in "Survival of the Classic." He informs us that he scrupulously avoided previous commentary until he had composed his own. (The legal analogy has obviously broken down.) And after he has read the book he makes no attempt to compare his own responses to those of other critics or to place the book among others of its kind. Instead he simply reports that on examining other criticism he found that no two readings saw it "as exactly alike" (*C*, 131). Out of this absence of unanimity, he legislates for a necessary plurality in the modern classic, which he now defines simply as a text that entertains "an extreme variety of response" (*C*, 118).

Kermode makes great claims for plurality, calling it a "requirement and a distinguishing feature of the survivor" (*C*, 133). In one sense he emphasizes plurality as a key element of the classic throughout his book, for without it Virgil can hardly have meant so many different things to so many different commentators. But toward the end the status of plurality subtly shifts. At the beginning, Kermode presents it simply as a means to the classic's survival; by the end it has become a value, a central point from which an ever-fluctuating classic takes its shape, a pointer to the necessary indeterminacy that secures the construction of new readings.

Like Eliot, Kermode is an imperialist in his relativism. And like Eliot too, he finally bases his conviction of the greatness of the classic on nothing more than faith. But Eliot's faith rests on Christian conviction, Kermode's on a kind of secular faith in the virtue of plurality. His classic exists in a vacancy belonging neither to past nor to present. Eliot's classic may exist only in eternity, but Kermode's can aspire at best to limbo. He has shriveled the most permanent and public of monuments to the point where it exists only as fragments in a solitary critic's consciousness.

V. INTERPRETATION

Although many reviewers thought that *The Classic* effected a valuable reconciliation between old models and new methodologies, a significant minority did not. Oliver Taplin saw the book as illuminating in parts but insidious in sum, for reasons that emerged only at the end when "Roland Barthes and Jacques Derrida are brought out from behind the arras. Yet," Taplin continued, "they are the powers behind the rostrum here, rather than Eliot, whose lecture 'What is a Classic?' provides little more than a nominal springboard for ideas which his ghost would, I suspect, disinherit." Along with Taplin, Gerald Graff and Quentin Anderson also objected strongly to the direction that Kermode's final pages took. Anderson thought his idea of the inexhaustible significance of the classic amounted to no more than a variant of the symbolist doctrine of the supreme value of art. "It is as if art had seeped into the place religion once occupied." Graff summed up the responses of all these critics when he spelled out the pedagogic and cultural consequences of Kermode's ideas. "He shares the predicament of numerous would-be defenders of 'continuities,' . . . 'ideas of order,' and 'humanistic values,' who see no way of getting beyond skeptical and nihilistic views of reality and history. Kermode's means of rescuing tradition by construing it as a subjective fiction only confirms the attacks of those who reject tradition as a consoling illusion."[1] Graff recognized a powerful strain of anti-rationalism in Kermode's book that encouraged reconstruction of the past according to ever-fluctuating present needs. In bringing the classic down to earth, Kermode succeeded only in burying it under an avalanche of ill-considered modern requirements. The humanistic cause needed more than an immediate and subjective basis if it were to prove a potent contemporary force.

As Graff and other reviewers suggest, from this point Kermode's career takes a more controversial turn. From the decade beginning in 1975, polemic becomes his chosen genre, controversy his very element. After the publication of *The Classic* he turns repeatedly to savage a host of opponents with the civilized elegance of his prose, and even essays that begin by promising to bring peace soon brandish the critical sword. The self-consciously "moderate" prologue to *The Art of Telling* (1983), a collection of essays written between 1971 and 1982, shows how unpredictable a peacemaker Kermode can be. His essay bristles with hostility toward the British academic and journalistic establishment (an odd position considering his own preeminence within both) and exhibits much rancor toward the unnamed traditionalists who "man the walls with their dusty banners: principle, imagination, the human world, though the most vocal of them are manifestly unacquainted with the first, lack the second and seem to know the third only by hearsay" (*AT*, 7). In this book, even the most routine academic exercise allows Kermode to ventilate his irritation. A review of the critical reception of E. M. Forster's *A Room with a View* leads him to reflect whether current reviewers "would do the job any better" than their not noticeably perceptive predecessors (*AT*, 11). Most of Kermode's antagonists go unnamed. At one point, however, seemingly unable to contain himself, he quotes Christopher Ricks's Polonian characterization of the "true reader and critic" who is "open-minded but not vacuous. . . . both independent and accessible." Kermode cannot conceal his scorn for words that "in pre-war 1966 . . . must have seemed almost too obvious or even banal to be worth the trouble of writing down" (*AT*, 8). However, in the way of occupying armies, Kermode uses Ricks's words to characterize his own criticism, which he oddly terms as working "from a position of moderation" (*AT*, 8). If, as his prologue states, "there is a war on," then one critic can certainly take care of himself.

Kermode's prologue focuses mainly on a local quarrel within the British literary establishment. Yet the book as a whole shows that this quarrel takes its place within a larger crisis of literary studies, a crisis in which Kermode himself has played a significant and much more problematic part. When Taplin, Anderson, and Graff attack *The Classic*, they do so as defenders of assumptions about authorial authority, the status of the text, and the rationality of its discourse that other critics—Kermode among them—had begun to question. The ferocity of the responses to *The Classic* suggests, indeed, a certain shift in Kermode's position. Virgil, Dante, and T. S. Eliot may stand at center stage; but behind the arras lurk Roland Barthes, Jacques Derrida, and Claude Levi-Strauss. Kermode's next two books, *The Genesis of Secrecy* (1979) and *The Art of Telling* (1983), indicate even more strongly his eagerness to assimilate the new theories to his own long-standing inquiry into the crisis of modernity, and to engage sustainedly with questions that had always fascinated him—authorial authority, institutional power, and the occult mysteries of the interpreter's art.

Kermode's intellectual development during the 1960s and the 1970s is best seen within the context of a movement that swept across the human sciences as a whole. In literary studies itself, student dissent and faculty demoralization had already by the mid-1960s provoked many calls for reform. Certainly, by 1969, when *New Literary History* unfurled its program for a new "journal of theory and interpretation," it implied that literary criticism risked extinction if it persisted in the claims for autonomy monumentalized in such canonical New Critical documents as René Wellek and Austin Warren's *Theory of Literature* (1948) and Cleanth Brooks and W. K. Wimsatt's *Literary Criticism: A Short History* (1957). In a manifesto that Kermode himself might have composed, the editor called for a renegotiated alliance between critic and historian based on a readjustment of "the relation between the theoretical and the practical, past interpretations and present needs." He hoped to encourage "a self consciousness and self examination" from literary critics, and he took the practical step of fostering them by soliciting contributions from philosophers and historians, who provided damaging evidence of the theoretical deficiencies in some of the standard literary histories.[2]

The impetus toward interdisciplinary study and a more rigorous theoretical foundation continued throughout this period. In 1974, Sheldon Sachs launched *Critical Inquiry* with the uncompromising testimony that the journal sought to promote "disciplined criticism." To that end, Sachs committed himself to

> the widest diversity of subject made generally interesting to advocates of disciplined criticism by our authors' concern for theory, method, and the exploration of critical principles. The literary critic who had no interest in E. H. Gombrich's *Art and Illusion*, the music critic who found Barbara Herrnstein Smith's *Poetic Closure* irrelevant to his concerns, the art historian who would simply be bored by Northrop Frye's *Anatomy of Criticism* or Karl Popper's *The Poverty of Historicism* were not our potential readers nor were meant to be.[3]

This sort of interdisciplinary inquiry could only lead to the adoption of new bearings for literary criticism. Increasingly, literary critics relinquished their judicial powers in order to understand the theoretical basis of their valuations. Instead of insisting on the primacy of literary language, they turned to speech-act theorists in order to understand its relationship to ordinary speech. Few new creative reputations were launched in these years, but the process of canon formation received intensive attention, while the old authorities on the canon looked increasingly insecure. Gone were the statutory allusions to Maritain or to Mr. Eliot. Literary students began to loosen their links with orthodoxy and to turn instead to figures like Ernst Gombrich, who described his aim in *Meditations on a Hobby Horse* (1963) as to study the history of art "like mathematics."[4]

During the same period, the impetus toward theory was fueled even more strikingly from quite another quarter. In 1966, the landmark eighth number of the French journal *Communications* provided evidence of a new critical avant-garde. The list of contributors included Roland Barthes, Claude Bremond, Umberto Eco, Gérald Genette, A. J. Greimas, Christian Metz, and Tzvetan Todorov, all of whom had written or would go on to write important theoretical works, some of them in Kermode's own field—narrative interpretation and the application of structuralist thinking to theological and literary texts. Later that same year, an international group of scholars met at Johns Hopkins to discuss "The Languages of Criticism and the Sciences of Man," and a whole intellectual revolution in Anglo-American criticism was under way.

By 1970, the proceedings of this symposium had been published as *The Languages of Criticism and the Sciences of Man: The Structuralist Controversy*. Two years later, the appearance of the volume in paperback as *The Structuralist Controversy* indicates the wider audience that the new theories now reached. Between 1966 and 1976, Anglo-American criticism took a novel turn. Jonathan Culler, Terence Hawkes, Frederic Jameson, and Robert Scholes provided introductions to structuralist thought. Translations of Barthes, Derrida, Foucault, Lacan, and Levi-Strauss were issued or reissued by American and British presses. Journals like *Diacritics* (1970), the *Oxford Literary Review* (1973), *Semiotexte* (1974), and *Glyph* (1977) emerged to propagate structuralist ideas. Finally, a group of distinguished American critics, including Harold Bloom, Geoffrey Hartman, Paul de Man, J. Hillis Miller, Stanley Fish, and Jonathan Culler, began to disseminate essays and monographs that ranged across the entire new critical field, embracing, sometimes in the same essay, structure and semiology, language and myth, politics and interpretation.

Structuralism and poststructuralism offered a bewildering abundance of possibilities. In the first place, they drastically altered the field that literary critics had customarily engaged. For if literature became a sub-system of language as a whole, the long isolation in the solitary consciousness that Kermode deplored in *Romantic Image* and *The Sense of an Ending* had ended at last. And if language itself could no longer be seen as the property of a single speaker or author, it became subject to the varying definitions and persuasions of readers situated within a series of conventional and institutional contexts. A literary text became an abyss rather than an object, an *écriture* that Barthes saw as a world where "everything is to be *disentangled*, nothing *deciphered*; the structure can be followed, 'run' (like the thread of a stocking) at every point and at every level, but there is nothing beneath: the space of writing is to be ranged over, not pierced; writing ceaselessly posits meaning ceaselessly to evaporate it, carrying out a systematic exemption of meaning."[5] Barthes replaced meaning with mystery and authors with texts, texts that no longer nested within a stable network of rational assumptions but "ran" uncontrollably up and down the whole ideological ladder.

During 1967, almost at the very beginning of these movements, Kermode launched his own contribution in the form of a regular seminar on narrative theory at University College, London. Even so, the record of his involvement in the new methods does not support the charge of absolute capitulation to French ideas that some British critics have leveled against him. In 1967, Kermode objected to Barthes's schismatic and even chauvinistic approach to modern literature as a distinctively French enterprise commencing in 1848. In the same article he commented unfavorably too on Levi-Strauss's "eerily fluent" style, which he saw as "only now and then making a simple statement." Unable at this point to concede the validity of this new "high intellectual fashion," he undertook in an essay of 1969 to show that by virtue of their narrative complexity and their sheer bulk, novels "are extremely resistant" to structuralist methods.[6]

In these early discussions, Kermode objected most strongly to the abstract, diagrammatic style of French structuralist thought, its way of reducing the complexities of narrative to a simplified, quasi-scientific structure. He did, however, come to respect the structuralists' self-consciously interpretative thrust, their bid, as he put it in 1981, "to illuminate the processes by which one knows" a literary text.[7] And in Barthes in particular he found an ally against what he saw as an incorrigibly provincial British literary establishment. Two lectures delivered in 1972, "Local and Provincial Restrictions" and "The Use of the Codes," clearly reflect both the influence of Barthes and Kermode's increasing willingness to explore narrative in more broadly theoretical terms. On both occasions, he insists that narratives call for active interpreters in order to achieve their full potential. "They will always invite us to plural glosses on the letter, to ingenious manipulation of the codes; it is their nature to demand that we produce rather than consume them, and that we liberate them from local and provincial restrictions, including, so far as that is possible, our own" (*AT*, 70–71). Kermode's long-standing interest in the activity of the reader reappears in these essays in brazenly theoretical dress, in a coat of many colors calculated to offend the more restricted. In *The Sense of an Ending* Kermode's reader was an enfeebled partner in the construction of fiction, a necessary but scarcely enthusiastic collaborator in the erection of minimalist monuments like Sartre's *Nausea* or Beckett's *How It Is*. But in *The Art of Telling* the same reader owes more to Wilde's dandy than to Beckett's clochard. Shedding his provinciality without restraint, Kermode declares his French liaisons overtly and accepts with gratitude the liberties they bring. The disconsolate tone of *The Sense of an Ending* and much of *The Classic* gives way to a flamboyant, self-conscious delight in the pleasures of the plural text.

It is hardly surprising that two years later, in 1974, Denis Donoghue represented Kermode to the readers of the new theoretical journal *Critical Inquiry* as a critic "engaged in a major study of fiction and the theory of fiction." If hardly a card-carrying member of *la nouvelle vague*, Kermode was clearly, in his own words, a "deeply interested reader."[8] But his interest is predictable, for the new developments offered him the liberty of interpretation that had fascinated him even in the 1950s. New methods, on occasions, had their complement in new subjects. Between 1972 and 1975 Kermode turned his attention to realistic fiction, detective novels, and French romances, while his later move into scriptural narrative also had its origins in these years. Modern thought made syncretism inescapable; like Coleridge, the modern critic must embrace the greatest variety of theories and ideas.

Between *The Sense of an Ending* and *The Classic*, Kermode's concern with interpretation made him, in Anglo-American circles at least, a virtual pioneer. Even so, at this stage his theoretical interests developed in a relatively informal and occasional manner. He merely took the opportunity, through the medium of a review or a lecture, to survey the conditions in which literary judgments and reputations are made. His various bids to assess the chances for the survival of the classic took this form. Even the lectures published as *The Classic* had something of the ad hoc property of work-in-progress about them. But by the late 1970s, Kermode could hardly maintain this kind of informality: to consider these issues at all was to participate in a well-marshaled debate not short of able spokesmen who raised important questions that ranged from the status of the text through the role of the reader to the nature of understanding itself. Moreover, in a British literary establishment notorious for its conservatism, Kermode had thrust on him the role of defender of the new. The result is some of his most powerful criticism, but also criticism that brings into prominence inconsistencies and contradictions that had previously remained latent in his work, contradictions that are latent in the whole notion of interpretation as he understands it.

Confronted by a text, a reader can perform one of several operations. He can scan it with the kind of attention that enables him to catch its drift. This is not a solution that commends itself to those who specialize in the understanding of texts—literary critics, lawyers, and others. When these readers confront their respective texts, they perform a variety of more professional operations. They may try to enter the text on the basis of an intuitive understanding that rests itself on their superior powers of sympathy or perception (though this is not a procedure of great appeal to lawyers), or they may try to recover the meaning of the words through research into similar texts, other works by the same author, or more general considerations of period, style, theme, or precedent. Both these operations accept that the original intentions of the author or the scribe must be honored; in both cases the critic offers a sophisticated variation on the verdict of the less diligent reader who affirms that the text means what it says.

But a third type of interpreter does not accept that the author's original intentions deserve privileged consideration. For this reader assumes that in so far as a text is composed of language, and in so far as language rests on a series of arbitrary relationships between signs, then the meaning of the text cannot be established with any certainty. From this, it is no great leap to the view that the text invites the reader to make his own kind of sense, which he produces by processing and codifying the clues the language offers. This type of interpreter lays himself open to the charge that he uses the text only as a starting point for his own meditations, a charge that he may fight off on a number of fronts.

When the vicar takes a text from scripture for his

Sunday sermon, he can engage in a variety of activities that calls for varying degrees of closeness to the words of his source. He may make the biblical text a basis for an appeal to his parishioners for pastoral assistance. He may subject a few words to prolonged analysis while ignoring their original context within the scripture. His concern about the message of the gospel may take him far away from its actual words. His interest in an overwhelming external context that inspired his sermon may make the text into an occasion for his eloquence on other matters. In recent years, literary critics have entertained the same range of options—and justifications—as the vicar in their attempts to press texts into significance for modern readers. They may emphasize the gap that time has opened up between the text's original and its current interpretations. They may insist that past and present significances be brought together as necessary components of any illuminating interpretation. Or they may scrutinize critically the interpretative institutions themselves, regarding their stewardship as an essential part of the text's continuing life.

Within this broad range of interpretative activity, two schools have recently squared off. On the one side, recognitive theorists like John Searle, Quentin Skinner, and Barbara Herrnstein Smith turn to speech-act and language theory for evidence that the language of the text, like the language of the marketplace, can be understood once its performative contexts are understood. On the other side, critics like Roland Barthes, Jacques Derrida, and J. Hillis Miller point to the testimony of Plato and Freud, authors who in varying ways allege that men always speak more than they understand. One group sees interpretation as a professional and rational activity; the other raises it to almost eschatological status. Following Heidegger, the last group turns interpretation into a brooding meditation on human knowledge. Can we trust our words? How do we know anything without knowing everything? As Paul Ricoeur has suggested, these are questions that make interpretation more an ontological than a textual matter. For some of the more radical poststructuralists, the very attempt to reconstruct an utterance involves a necessary compliance with the repressive and the authoritarian.

Although Kermode himself has never endorsed so extreme a position (he has written that "the attempt to reconstruct a past response . . . is, for most of us, an important element in all acceptable interpretation" [*AT*, 28]), he has not held back in his attacks on the other side. He presents the intentionalist case as a "silencer of the imagination" (*AT*, 199) and the recognitive theorists as antiquarians standing "where biblical critics stood in the 1740s" (*AT*, 125). Even so, he does not usually discuss these issues in the abstract but rather pins his theoretical statements to some specific inquiry, a procedure that allows him to present himself in the manner of I. A. Richards, as a critic who employs empirical methods as a springboard for more hermetic investigations. The new insistence on indeterminacy proves, he thinks, that "literary theory has now caught up with common sense" (*AT*, 128). In the thick of the present literary crisis he calls for "a great man who might, like Eliot, hold together the new and the traditional, catastrophe and continuity" (*AT*, 7). In *The Art of Telling*, *The Genesis of Secrecy* (1979), and his uncollected essays of the 1970s and the 1980s, Kermode continues to write in his own traditional mode, straddling the centuries, yoking Chrétien de Troyes to Michel Butor, George Eliot to Peter Handke, and, most audaciously of all, the Gospel of Saint Mark to a variety of modern fictions including James Joyce's *Ulysses*, Henry Green's *Party Going*, and Thomas Pynchon's *The Crying of Lot 49*. Such exercises in reconciliation hint at Eliot-like intentions of the sort apparent in *The Classic*. But does Kermode "hold together" the forces he juggles or merely disintegrate them in ever more interesting ways?

Despite its author's catholicity, *The Art of Telling* hinges on a highly specialized position, that "the modern critical tradition, for all its variety, has one continuous element, the search for occulted sense in texts of whatever period" (*AT*, 24). In Kermode's view, the typical modern reader moves "from one part of the text to another, rather than to some intelligible world without" (*AT*, 16). The analogy is to music, which mysteriously confers "a larger existence" on the auditor (*AT*, 12). Like E. M. Forster, Kermode speaks of signals that realize the text's "indications of larger history" and "full possibility of meaning" (*AT*, 25). In an eloquent coda, he describes the history of criticism as a series of attempts "to earn the privilege of access to that kingdom of the larger existence which is in our time the secular surrogate of another Kingdom whose horizon is no longer within our range" (*AT*, 31–32).

In language and implication, Kermode's work in this period suggests the continuing influence in his thought of the symbolist aesthetics that some critics detected behind *Romantic Image*. *The Art of Telling* celebrates an uncertain kingdom not of systematic *correspondances* but of intermittent illuminations. Its vehicle is the novel rather than the lyric. It is skeptical and auditory rather than absolute and visionary. But its destination, a "larger existence" denied to outsiders deaf to secret senses and latent properties, reconstructs for readers of the 1970s and the 1980s an older symbolist case.

Unfortunately, few symbolists committed themselves to the second part of Kermode's program, the reconciliation of old and new, institutional and heretic. And the inescapably schismatic, anti-historical thrust of a symbolist poetic also makes its mark on the pages that Kermode devotes to this. In fact, his own work exhibits the typically symbolist fallacies he annihilated in *Romantic Image*. Like the poets described in that book, he proceeds by a series of polarizations (between kinds of reader, types of text, and forms of interpretation) and then moves to large scale syntheses that give current needs the sanction of history.

However conciliatory in his intentions, Kermode always elevates his highly specialized occult mode of reading over any opposition. At one point he pauses to offer conciliatory words to the common reader, observing that one should not "despise the naive reading so completely," only to hurry on to the remark that "it involves an unconscious complicity with arbitrary authority" (*AT*, 112). At another point he concedes that realistic fiction has its own norms and expectations, only to suggest that it also betrays "a nostalgia for the types, an anachronistic myth of common understanding and shared universes of meaning" (*AT*, 103). Kermode's own interests clearly lie beyond the pleasures of conformity and common understanding. His own preferred area is one where "we mortals stand alone," knowing that "to make sense of reality the mind must work with all its powers" (*AT*, 103). He admires the way narrative undermines accepted half-truths, mocking the "pretense that everybody can agree on a particular construction of reality" (*AT*, 112). He accepts gratefully the way narrative throws every reader on his own resources with its "secret invitations to interpretation rather than appeals to a consensus" (*AT*, 144). And he delights in the consequence of these subversions, the hint that "it is possible to live, because it is possible to read, without accepting official versions of reality" (*AT*, 70).

Given the self-consciously heretical principles that Kermode expounds, one can see why his account of interpretative institutions in two important essays of 1977 and 1979 becomes so confusing. In "Can We Say Absolutely Anything We Like?" and "Institutional Control of Interpretation," both reprinted in *The Art of Telling*, Kermode offers extended discussions of the rules, roles, and responsibilities of institutions devoted to the interpretation of literary texts. His ambition is to reconcile his solitary, occult poetics of narrative with a criticism devoted to the transmission of cultural values and the certification of professional skills. In the first essay he uses Michael Polanyi's essentially conservative idea of "tacit knowledge" to show how institutions rule out ingenious but fallacious interpretations. Without this kind of knowledge any institution would need to think out its basic principles every day. A similar conservatism underpins the second essay, which shows, through an extended analogy with the church, how institutions select texts for study, regulate teaching methods, and monitor the admission of those permitted to study them. Basic to each essay is Kermode's conviction that an unbridgeable divide separates specialists and lay practitioners and that the sole agent of the text's continued existence is the "spiritual" reading of the expert. His own practice as a reviewer for more than three decades hardly supports the division he invokes.

The symbolist critic is always weak on questions of power and ideology, and it is here, predictably enough, that Kermode's discussion of interpretative institutions first founders. When he surveys the multitude of radical approaches—black, feminist, Marxist—that are currently practiced, he cannot escape the complacency that is the reverse side of the symbolist coin. "This is not the place to enter into discussion of the validity of such new doctrine; I should . . . merely ask how we may expect the institution to contain or control it." Kermode allows subversion to operate within fixed boundaries; he relies on "control of appointments and promotions" (*AT*, 181) to absorb any ideological excess. The result is a theory of institutional change that resembles an odd conjunction of Dale Carnegie and Villiers's Axël.

Nor does he seem eager to examine directly the actual mechanisms of institutional change. In typical symbolist fashion he proceeds analogically, comparing the literary community with institutions scientific, clerical, and psychoanalytical. Like scientists, literary critics regulate the admission and the interpretation of evidence. Like the clergy, they establish a canon and then fix approved ways of reading it. Like psychoanalysts, they focus on the latent as much as the manifest. Yet all these analogies do not add up to a concrete characterization of an interpretative community in its specific social, psychological, and intellectual contexts. With something like distaste, Kermode confesses that "if we wanted to describe its actual social existence we should get involved in a complex account of its concrete manifestations in universities, colleges, associations of higher learning; and if we wanted to define its authority we should have to consider not only its statutory right to confer degrees and the like, but also the subtler forms of authority acquired and exercised by its senior and more gifted members" (*AT*, 168–69). The slide from "senior" to "more gifted" indicates Kermode's assumptions. His is a hermeneutics addressed to the sultans, not to the janissaries or the young turks.

Because he sees the basis of literary studies as the cultivation of the occult, Kermode can offer little information about the daily contingencies by which texts are canonized, skills are transmitted, and careers are made and lost. Even so, he seems unwilling to present any of these issues as unimportant, and as a result he glosses over the specific interpretative duties he feels compelled to discuss. In a symbolist hermeneutics it is, of course, the interpreter, not the interpretative institution, that occupies center stage. Yet the Kermode of *The Art of Telling* remains far from clear about the interpreter's calling, sometimes devoting him exclusively to the manifestation of the occult, but on other occasions confining him to more mundane chores such as the training of the young. In "On Reading Novels," for instance, he says that the young should be taught "what it is that 'holds a book together.'" A course in interpretation "involves the divination of generic expectations and structures; it requires you to know what educated people know, and is therefore a pleasure of conformity" (*AT*, 130). On the one side he characterizes the academy as an institution that is endlessly accommodating. (He describes it at one point as "genteel, Anglican, and pluralistic" [*AT*, 163].) On the other side he confronts us with an institution that is, by definition, exclusionist. "Like the masters who reserved secret senses in the second century," he suggests, "we are in the business of conducting readers out of the sphere of the manifest" (*AT*, 182). If the *we* here represents a typical member of the interpretative institution, he would have to reconcile the very different talents of Goldsmith's Dr. Primrose and Hermes Trismegistus.

*   *   *

But Kermode's own intellectual energies scarcely suggest the virtues of the former, for he repeatedly emphasizes the need to discover the occult senses latent in any text. To discover the "secrets lurking in the tale-bearing text" is to enter into typically "modern modes of interpretation, continuous with older ones and yet proper to their epoch" (*AT*, 31). Kermode claims, moreover, that participation in the modern interpretative process "ought to change conventional attitudes to all, and not merely new, texts" (*AT*, 65). His own extended bid to change these attitudes came in 1979 with the publication of *The Genesis of Secrecy*, a major contribution to the rediscovery of this occult interpretative tradition. *The Genesis of Secrecy* typically combines modern concerns with old texts, in this case a text with a significant history of interpretation behind it, the Gospel of Saint Mark. Such a text enjoys the status of a sacred classic, a combination that Kermode could hardly be expected to resist. But like the modern classics that Kermode so much admires, Mark also has its puzzles—obliquities and abruptnesses that alarmed its commentators for many years. The uniquely favorable conjunction of a hallowed but obscure text and a solid history of interpretation characterized by fluctuating assessments of the status and the value of the interpreted work presents unique possibilities for Kermode's investigation of "interpretations . . . their modes, their possibilities, and their disappointments" (*GS*, 133).

In his choice of Mark, Kermode typically lit upon a text that earlier interpreters did not much value. Augustine's verdict that Mark offered an inferior redaction of Matthew set the course for the general conviction of Mark's inferiority that prevailed for centuries. Only when nineteenth-century scholars began to argue that Matthew derived from Mark did the seeds of revaluation get planted. Yet even then commentators proceeded cautiously, resting the Gospel's value on its documentary virtues. Vincent Taylor, author of the standard modern commentary on Mark, has continued in this older interpretative tradition. For instance, his reading of the parable of the wicked husbandmen (12:1–12) suggests that the text is allegorical only in a highly controlled and specific way. "No allegorical significance belongs to the hedge, the pit, the wine press, the tower, the other country, the fruit, the exterior of the vineyard; in short, the narrative is not pure allegory."[9] Taylor's conservatism has a long history that goes as far back as the second century, when Tertullian's *De Pudicitia* stated, "We prefer to find less meaning in the Bible, if possible, rather than the opposite."[10]

Yet a rival tradition has almost as long a history and has particular interest in relation to Kermode. Deriving from Philo Judaeus and Christian Platonists like Origen and Clement of Alexandria, this mode of interpretation tried "to ignore the literal sense and to concentrate upon a meaning which was as far as possible from the plain, surface meaning taken in its context."[11] Thus Clement's interpretation of the parable of the good samaritan pressed every element of the story, from its characters to its properties, into allegorical service. This method tended to destroy the parable's narrative continuity, replacing it with a commentary that "undertook to comment upon every phrase, indeed on almost every word, of the text dealt with."[12]

Two interpretative traditions, then, exist in scriptural history. One moves the gospels toward documentary, the other toward allegory. One relates the gospels to the needs of the Christian community for whom the apostles are presumed to have written, the other to the need of later Christians for a perpetual purchase on the revelations of scripture. There are obvious similarities in these positions to the debate about the artist's intentions and the text's occult properties outlined in the section above. But an interpreter of Mark in particular must also confront a third problem, for this is the epitome of an outsider's text, whose dark narrative and disquieting implications have long resisted official interpreters. In this text, Jesus repeatedly hints at purposes neither pastoral nor eschatological. For instance, at 4:12 he explains that he speaks to his disciples in parables "that seeing they may see, and not perceive; and hearing they may hear, and not understand; lest at any time they should be converted, and their sins should be forgiven them." Taylor calls these words "intolerable," since they deny his conviction that "the purpose of parabolic teaching . . . is to elucidate truth, not to obscure it."[13] To extricate himself from this problem he invokes textual history. The "strong Palestinian flavour" of Jesus's remark suggests that originally the saying "probably had nothing to do with parables at all" but became garbled in the transmission.[14] In scriptural commentary, history customarily serves as a check on interpretative excess. Here a conjectural history resting heavily on idiom eases the text out of an ideological knot that may even have involved a reassessment of Jesus's mission.

Mark studs his gospel with silences that call for interpretative intervention. And at the end he offers no announcement of good news, no miraculous reappearance, only words that violate grammar and test belief. He describes how the women who come to Jesus's tomb see only a young man "clothed in a long white garment." Charged by him to go to Galilee, where they will find Jesus, "they went out quickly, and fled from the sepulchre; for they trembled and were amazed: neither said they anything to any man; for they were afraid" (16:8). This strangely inconclusive ending has elicited much interpretative ingenuity. An unknown hand provided the Gospel with eleven extra verses. Some commentators hypothesize about a missing portion of manuscript; others conjecture that the apostle died before his work reached completion.

As a self-confessed outsider, Kermode can observe these activities with a certain impartiality. In a spirit of hermeneutical ecumenicism, he attempts to unite conservative and allegorical interpreters around a common goal. "If there is one belief (however the facts resist it) that unites us all, from the evangelists to those who argue away inconvenient portions of their texts, and those who spin large plots to accommodate the discrepancies and dissonances into some larger scheme, it is this conviction that somehow, in some occult fashion, if we could only detect it, everything will be found to hang together" (GS, 72). Kermode wants to distinguish his own tolerant pluralism from a conservative tradition that he sees as excessively eager to explain away narrative obliquity and from a schismatic sectarianism that he sees as utopian in its quest for universal significances. His own position he offers, predictably enough, as a mediating one.

His desire to steer a middle course between exegetical excess and documentary austerity, between the reading that fragments the text into a thousand possibilities and the reading that sees it only as the record of a single community on one unique occasion, leads Kermode to the work of Austin Farrer, a twentieth-century British scholar and divine. In *Spenser and the Allegorists* (1962), Kermode argued that Farrer's methods entailed "a total rejection of history" (*SSD*, 30). However, in *The Genesis of Secrecy*, he welcomes Farrer as one who "makes bold to write about Mark as another man might write about Spenser" (GS, 72). Pursuing Farrer's trail, Kermode discovers in Mark a text wrapped in complex incongruities, subtle obliquities, failed fulfillments, and narrative indirections. Happy to concede the possibility of authorial intentions provided these intentions are nested in a text of sufficient complexity, Kermode uncovers a text veritably modern in its obscurity. Mark's gospel resembles *Ulysses* in the promise of fulfillment it tantalizingly fails to provide. It recalls *The Crying of Lot 49* in reducing history to a chamber of fading echoes. And at its ending it recalls *Finnegans Wake* in its aposiopesis or *The Magic Mountain* in its unwillingness to console its audience.

Kermode thinks that Mark hangs together in the same way as these modern occult narratives. He responds with an almost equally occult prose poem to "the splendors and miseries" of an interpreter confronted by a dark and obscure text (*GS*, 122). A network of violent imagery opens his book, underscoring the rough magic of the interpreter's art, the "violence and stealth" by which a modern practitioner assumes "the interpretative inadequacy" of those that precede him (*GS*, 1, 5, 17). Like Eliot in *Four Quartets*, Kermode repeatedly provides a wry commentary on his own performance. To stress the utter tentativeness of his interpretations, he frequently doubles his phrases. For instance he describes our interpretations of stories in terms of "our perhaps delusive sense of their perhaps delusive radiance" (*GS*, 99). He clinches his conviction about the provisionality of our commitment to order with a similar doubled formulation: "we all seek the center that will allow the senses to rest, at any rate for one interpreter, at any rate for one moment" (*GS*, 72). Once again Kermode introduces a skeptical note into what initially seemed so stable. And at the end of the book, the tentativeness of the writer melts into the obscurity of the universe itself, as a cluster of images of vision and blindness, light and dark emphasizes the only sporadic illumination any interpreter enjoys. Blind men, intermittent radiances "gleaming unearthly white," "deafness and blindness" (*GS*, 143): the last pages move into a world of complete incertitude.

> Mystery and stupidity make an important conjunction or opposition; but it must be seen with all the others, denial and recognition, silence and proclamation, clean and unclean, indoors and out, lake and mountain, one side and the other side. Even the apocalypse is both now, and

to come. And we know that at the end of the book the resurrection is proclaimed to those who keep silence, from a place that is within doors yet open, since the stone has been rolled back; it is a tomb but it contains an unrecognized young man who reminds us of the one who ran away; he is not naked, like the demoniac in his tombs, but civilly clothed, like the demoniac cured; in a place normally unclean but now clean he proclaims, he does not shriek. This mystery is confronted with stupid silence. (*GS*, 143)

Kermode avails himself of the stage machinery of structuralist criticism, but the overall effect of his prose owes more to Samuel Beckett than to Roland Barthes. The bare landscape and the elusive young man recall the last scenes of *Waiting for Godot*, with the well-dressed demoniac playing an unrecognized sibling of Lucky. Like some latter day Pirandello, Kermode recasts the biblical drama with a sequence of baffled protagonists: a Peter whose "silliness" makes him "bustle about building . . . shelters"; and a James and a John who "had seen but not perceived, heard but not understood" (*GS*, 143). Like Kafka, Kermode takes his protagonists to the very threshold of understanding, where he leaves them without reassuring certitude. The battery of self-canceling abstractions, the mute and estranged environment, the confident young demoniac all serve to rip the veneer of conventionality from the gospel. Kermode does not simply write *about* uncertainty: he actually tries to wrap us inside it.

Like his own chosen deity Hermes, Kermode crosses boundaries recklessly. One boundary he passes quite gracefully is the time-honored barrier between criticism and creation. But other boundaries remain, and here Kermode's crossings seem less felicitous. His ideas of order, like Austin Farrer's, are aesthetic. But unlike Kermode, Farrer supplements his aesthetic convictions with the belief that "if we allow the evangelist to tell us his story in his own 'theological' or 'symbolical' way, and do not interpose with premature questions based on our own ideas of historical enquiry, we may be able to discern a genuine history which is communicated to us through the symbolism and not in defiance of it."[15] As Kermode's own book progresses, any accommodation between history and narrative becomes ever more remote, with the relationship between world and book seen as "endlessly disappointing" (*GS*, 145). In *The Genesis of Secrecy*, order itself becomes at best a symbolic construct; and beyond order Kermode sees only the unfathomability of history and the fictiveness of reality as a whole.

In *The Sense of an Ending*, Kermode staked his whole enterprise on the human capacity to entertain the fictive alongside the real in a dissonance that proved productive for both. But in *The Genesis of Secrecy*, it seems impossible for him to achieve this difficult concord. "The more complex the purely literary structure is shown to be, the harder it is for most people to accept the narratives as naively transparent upon historical reality" (*GS*, 62). It remains less than clear how the Kermode who only five years before unequivocally rejected "the pretense that everybody can agree on a particular construction of reality" (*AT*, 112) can now take upon himself to speak for "most people." As so often, Kermode's style dangles before his reader a consensus that his words brutally whip away.

In the last chapters of his book, Kermode's inquiry moves beyond Mark into other gospels and narratives. In "What Precisely Are the Facts?," he juxtaposes the crucifixion narrative in the Gospel of Saint John with a passage from Pynchon's *The Crying of Lot 49*. In both texts he finds a pseudo-historical narrative woven from other texts: in the evangelist, from Old Testament prophecy; in Pynchon, from his characters' own crazy guesswork. Pynchon shows how a possibly apocryphal encounter between Russian and American forces off the coast of California becomes for the characters in the story the source of a whole sectarian cult. Kermode does not exactly spell out the implications of this for Christianity, but, almost as damagingly, he uses the sectarian universe of Pynchon's novel to throw doubt on history and on narrative alike. "As we read on the question arises, whether we do not live in a complex of semiotic systems which are either empty or are operated on the gratuitous assumption that a direct relation exists between a sign and a corresponding object 'in reality'" (*GS*, 108). By a now familiar sleight of hand, Kermode moves from a tolerant pluralism to an eclectic relativism. As he drapes his skepticism over everything he encounters, an aesthetic and ultimately symbolic idea of order reduces history to one of the less interesting fictions.

Kermode thinks that history writing, unlike the more complex fictions of the interpreter, relies on "the myth of transparency" (*GS*, 118). The authority of historical narrative depends on the daily torpor that permits men to comply with still emptier fictions. As long as everything hangs together in some sort of order, the grossest lie will find plenty of takers:

> we mostly go about our business as if the contrary of what we profess to believe were the truth; somehow, from somewhere, a privilege, an authority descends upon our researches; and, as long as we do things as they have generally been done—as long, that is, as the institution which guarantees our studies upholds the fictions that give them value—we shall continue to write historical narrative as if it were an altogether different matter from making fictions, or *a fortiori*, from telling lies. (*GS*, 109)

Kermode has evidently drifted from a tolerant acceptance of a variety of ordering fictions toward an implicit claim for his own interpretative powers. *He* does not proceed with this benign sloth; *he* sees behind and beneath the text that others mouth unthinkingly.

Yet one wonders whether any historian actually writes a "historical narrative" in the way that Kermode describes. By taking the xenophobic and irrational world of Pynchon's characters as a model for the historian, Kermode typically blends together two entirely different frames of reference. Unlike Pynchon, the typical historian seeks to reconstruct events according to shared rational norms of causality and sequence. An historical archivist will hardly sympathize with the armchair skepticism that Pynchon's narrative parodies. According to G. R. Elton in *The Practice of History*, the historian conducts instead "an exhaustive, and exhausting, review of everything that may conceivably be germane to a given investigation."[16] The novelist, like the exegete, attends to what is written and may, if he wishes, confine himself to the internal features of a text. The historian scrutinizes what is written about, the larger world that the text looks out upon. Kermode himself remains free to do either or both, but he surely ought not to collapse the latter activity into the former or to suggest that the historian composes his narrative according to the most dogmatic kind of institutional norms. Not every historian is a Eusebius. In his bid to expand the authority of the interpreter's vision, Kermode devalues other forms of rational inquiry.

Moreover, he effectively closes the book of the past. For all the brilliance of its meditations, *The Genesis of Secrecy* consolidates Kermode's tendency toward the most inward-turning critical inquiry. All too inevitably, the Gospel according to Kermode turns into a problem of interpretation. What he calls "the modern mode of interpretation" reflects itself back to us across the centuries, so that a method aimed at fusing horizons replays only a permanent sense of the present. Perhaps this represents the largest disappointment of the interpreter's art, that it can only reproduce so many dazzling ways of talking about one problem. *The Genesis of Secrecy* makes an outstanding contribution to a critical crisis that it never satisfactorily resolves. By insisting on an "occult" level of interpretation, Kermode threatens to polarize the critical community even further, not to reunite it.

VI. CONCLUSION

THE combination of elegiac sentiments and up-to-the-minute speculation that characterizes the final chapters of *The Genesis of Secrecy* hints at divided allegiances in Kermode's thinking. Yet these ambivalences are hardly new to his criticism. In *Romantic Image* he simultaneously uncovered a hermetic tradition and demolished an official mythology. In *The Sense of an Ending* he took an aesthetic instrument, the fiction, to the historian's task of "making sense of the way we make sense of our lives." And in *The Classic* he tried simultaneously to understand the past in its own right and to make it perpetually new.

The past and the modern relationship to the past have always provided Kermode's central topics. What do Eliot and Pound, who acknowledged only the most remote of their ancestors, owe to closer progenitors like Wordsworth and Blake? How far are contemporary notions of crisis conditioned by imagery inherited from Christian apocalypse? Such are the questions that Kermode, a self-styled historian, "a diachronic sort of person" (*AT*, 5), and an incorrigible synthetist of old and new, has always tried to answer. But his latest synthesis, of French semiotics and scriptural narrative, ends by abolishing the historical crisis that provided his point of departure. In *The Genesis of Secrecy*, Kermode looks on a world consisting of nothing more than a network of codes and ideologies. The critic who began his career as a student of the modern by destroying the historicity of the myth of dissociation now sees history itself dissolve into a series of mythologies and coercive fictions.

At the same time that he became caught in the crisis between history and narrative, Kermode stumbled on yet another crisis in the humanities. Reviewing Tony

Tanner's *Adultery in the Novel* (1980), he praised the author highly. In its willingness to ransack the text for "the unread places . . . [where] one finds the intimate consonance, the surprising secret, the significant transgression," the book raised the interpretation of narrative to new heights. Yet Kermode ruefully acknowledged that Tanner "reminds us of another contract, and transgresses it. I mean the old contract between critic and reader . . . which was founded on the assumption that although the writer was likely to be better informed on the particular subject, he and the reader were essentially the same kind of person, similarly educated, and likely to be brought to agreement, or left in informed disagreement, by a familiar, sanctioned mode of discourse." No such informed consensus underwrote Tanner's own inquiry, which led the study of narrative to a new level of sophistication only to obscure it from the common view. Kermode viewed this "new transgressive criticism"—to which he himself made a significant contribution just six months earlier in his fine essay on Conrad's *Under Western Eyes*—with some suspicion, asking "whether this remarkable book . . . will ever make much contribution to the common wisdom."[1]

In a curious way, Kermode's investigation of the modern returned in 1980 to its point of origin. In 1957 he wrote a study of modern poetry pointing out the cost of a tradition built on an antithesis between the poetic imagination and ordinary reality. In 1980 he faced the problem of a critical vanguard moving ever further from the language and the concerns of the ordinary reading public. The battles of modernism endlessly repeated themselves. Fought once by High Modernist writers like Yeats and Joyce, fought a second time by latter-day schismatics like Burroughs and Ginsberg, the battle between avant-garde and public raged once more among the ranks of contemporary critics.

Kermode's own responses to this critical crisis have been intriguingly ambivalent. Readers of the *London Review of Books* will frequently have noticed his exasperation at leading British critics unwilling to welcome the latest continental and American developments. In his role as a propagandist for the new, Kermode can sound like an updated F. R. Leavis, with Dame Helen Gardner or Graham Hough acting as his unfortunate substitutes for Edith Sitwell or Lord David Cecil. But if Kermode has given no quarter in his quarrels with what he sees as an insular critical tradition, the old guard of British critics has perhaps influenced his position more than he might concede, since his latest essays show considerable awareness of the needs of a nonspecialist public and present criticism as a social institution as much as a hermetic calling.

Two lectures given at the beginning of the 1980s pinpoint the shift in Kermode's attitudes. In "Secrets and Narrative Sequence," a talk delivered at a Chicago symposium on narrative in October 1979 and reprinted in *The Art of Telling*, he presented one of his most dazzlingly occult exercises in interpretation. But in "The Decline of the Man of Letters," a lecture delivered to the American Academy in February 1983, he called for a critical realignment. "What the profession of letters requires is a new version of that blend of interests and assumptions that marked the bookman." Kermode addressed the Academy not on the tormented Joseph Conrad who figured in the Chicago lecture and whose *Under Western Eyes* cost him a breakdown, but on Arnold Bennett, a figure like Hermes—deity for merchants as well as interpreters—in his ability to turn the profession of letters into a highly profitable career. Kermode's championship of this unlikely figure testifies to his willingness to move from "the masters who reserved the secret senses" to a realignment with a larger literary public. Where his first lecture presented writing and interpreting as subversive activities, his second lecture discusses them as transmissible and humane skills. This lecture ends not with Conrad prophesying his own failure but with Arnold Bennett, an "eager lamplit figure, unpacking his century of classics, opening the *Juvenal*, and remembering—with felicitous inaccuracy—those lines from *Philaster*."[2] The pleasures of the lecture are of recognition not deception, as Kermode endeavors, somewhat in the manner of a nineteenth-century historical novelist, to conjure up the picture of a vanished age.

Kermode's most recent book tries to recapture still more of Bennett's territory. *Forms of Attention* (1985), a collection of the Wellek Library lectures given at the University of California, Irvine, demonstrates the intellectual pluralism that *The Genesis of Secrecy* and *The Art of Telling* called for but seldom exhibited. Kermode's subject is, once again, the survival of the classic, which happens in a different way in each of the cases he discusses. In the first lecture, "Botticelli Recovered," Kermode follows the method of "The Decline of the Man of Letters" and relates an absorbing historical narrative about the survival of Botticelli. His discussion shows how this classic has survived as a providential gift. In Kermode's story, chance discovers Botticelli, while uninformed enthusiasm sustains him. Only finally does scholarly knowledge, in the shape of the formidable Herbert Horne and the erudite and speculative Aby Warburg, arrive to consolidate the artist's place in the canon. Kermode's powers as a storyteller emerge as considerable. He is a master of characterization and setting, rendering an intimate portrait of the stiff and repressed Horne with a few of the novelist's easy strokes as "a surly, even sinister figure, a successful but dispassionate womanizer, and a secret homosexual" (*FA*, 7), and representing the milieu of London in the 1890s with a chronicler's authenticity as a world where "respectable clergymen as well as artists and professors waited for dancing girls in back alleys, since the ritual required it" (*FA*, 9). But the shift in perspective goes beyond Kermode's tone. He makes a romance out of Botticelli's whole survival as a classic, with the artist cast as a romantic hero rescued from an "oblivion . . . close to being total" (*FA*, 3) by a providence that elects him to "a position of eminence" (*FA*, 6) in a canon that secures him from the ruins of time.

Kermode's second lecture, "Cornelius and Voltemand: Doubles in *Hamlet*," revisits a Shakespearean classic in a manner that recalls his earlier lecture "Survival of the Classic." Yet the present lecture has none of the existential edge that animated his earlier discussion of *King Lear*. Kermode no longer feels he has to tease out the text's properties as an "obsessed" and "reticent" object. Since entry into the canon provides delivery from time, the status of *Hamlet* is assured. Kermode need not reimagine the unique grounds of the play's existence back into life as in the crisis-ridden 1960s. Instead, he can say something new by the less drastic means of "an attempt to marginalize what had been the central interest of many generations of *Hamlet*, and to put in the central position an aspect of the play that had been regarded as merely peripheral" (*FA*, 92). In this formulation generational changes in the life of the classic become spatial rather than ideological. Kermode's lecture discusses the play as a family romance, finding in it a meditation on the mysteries of identity and the relationship between substance and shadow. His interpretation does not originate in an heroic attempt to arrive at a generation's *Hamlet* (as his earlier lecture had undertaken to correct a generation's *Lear*) but in a simple need to sustain a critical conversation. Kermode attaches much importance to such conversation, since "the medium in which [the classic] survives is commentary" (*FA*, 36).

Kermode's last lecture, "Disentangling Knowledge from Opinion," surveys the current crisis among commentators. Do the multiple versions of any text that modern criticism invariably offers damage its integrity as an object of value? He does not think that this is necessarily the case and argues that the classic text subsists through the interpretations that constitute the "conversation" around it. But even for Kermode this idea is not absolutely new. In a review of Marshall McLuhan in 1964 he remarked on how our "new view of new views" leads to new illuminations. "We see that we shall get our answers from a study of the tools and agencies rather than from the 'material.'"[3] And in *Forms of Attention* he speaks well too of Aby Warburg's habit of using "other men's thoughts and systems of ideas as stimulants rather than as schemes he might or might not adopt . . . for the stimulus that might give rise to a brainwave of his own" (*FA*, 20).

Kermode's own methods in these two lectures clearly owe much to Warburg. Borrowing from the historical scholarship of Michael Levey, the biographical skills of Iain Fletcher and E. H. Gombrich, the rhetorical criticism of George T. Wright, and displaying a layman's interest in psychoanalysis, Kermode provides an empirical demonstration of the value of eclecticism. But his last talk extends his chosen method into something between a theory and a fiat, for in his closing remarks his eclecticism takes an almost mystical turn.

> Whatever takes the part of virtue against fortune, whatever preserves and restores some object of which the value may have been or may be in danger of getting lost is, however prone to error, good. So Warburg's phobic engrams are good, and so are the allegorizations of the Song of Songs and the now institutionalized "readings" of *Ulysses*, and the myths of heterocosm or the dissociation of sensibility. Also, the arguments against all these things can be good. What is not good is anything whatever that might destroy the objects valued or their value, or divert from them the special forms of attention they have been accorded. (*FA*, 92)

The tone of these valedictory remarks belongs more to the providential world of romance than to the quotidian world of literary criticism. For where outside a world guaranteed by providence can a multiplicity of opposite opinions coexist and each receive a blessing? In his third lecture, Kermode alleges that classics exist beyond time and that he himself can survey critical opinions from the same timeless vantage point. Yet classics and criticism exist alike as acts of rational choice. Does Kermode abdicate the critic's prerogative of choice for a world where everything hangs together for the best? His words recall Yvor Winters's biting characterization of T. S. Eliot. "At any given time he can speak . . . on both sides of almost any question."[4]

It may seem churlish to quarrel with the hand of friendship that Kermode extends in these pages. Yet surely he is elevating a condition of modern criticism—its ability to cite almost any authority for almost any opinion—into a prescription for its ills. By an almost Prospero-like feint he abdicates authority by blessing all comers, while retaining it by pronouncing them good provided they do the classic no harm. But what actually are the grounds by which good or harm can be done? Kermode's discussion leaves no way of deciding this, since he allows equal validity to all perspectives that critical attention could conceivably bring.

It is difficult to see how the omnisignificance that Kermode ascribes to the classic, its ability to yield meanings from any critical perspective, can translate into a serious program for the critic. Kermode's emphasis on "forms of attention" removes both text and critic from history, suspending both in a void where old critical battles about Othello's nobility and Lady Macbeth's children have to be fought all over again by readers bent on discovering them for the first time. There is something saintly in the tolerance that Kermode extends to all forms of critical discourse in his refusal to disentangle opinion from knowledge. Even so it is worth remembering that literary criticism has not customarily provided a sanctuary for saints but has been conducted by and on behalf of men speaking to—and arguing with—men. And the medium for their arguments has been time, not the *aevum* from which Kermode, now seeing as angels see, views the business of criticism in his final pages.

In a curious way, Kermode's career has in *Forms of Attention* turned full circle, back to the Abraham Cowley on whom he began an M.A. thesis after the war. This most metaphysical of modern critics continued in 1985 to deploy his wit and learning to reconcile the opposing factions of modern thought. Indeed, his keen eye for the schisms that threaten to disintegrate the modern sensibility has sharpened as his career has continued. In *Romantic Image* he recorded the split between artistic consciousness and common understanding. In *The Sense of an Ending* he meditated on the gap between the long perspectives of Christian history and the impoverished views available to the modern. In his ambitious book *The Classic* he tried to mediate between the Virgilian classic that linked time and eternity in one significant movement and the modern classic that survived by virtue of its indeterminacy. The major impulse in his later works, *The Genesis of Secrecy* and *The Art of Telling*, was to reconcile the interpreter's two rival necessities: the need to liberate the secret subtext; and the need to educate a fresh generation of interpreters.

Unfortunately, Kermode's refusal to commit himself unequivocally to any of the orthodoxies or heresies he examines makes him one of the hardest postwar critics to place. Allegiances as tentative as his do not supply the kind of signposts on which the commentator usually relies. In fact, it is much easier to record the list of roads Kermode has not taken than to assess precisely where he stands. He has not, for example, confined himself to one period, like Meyer Abrams, or to one method, like Wayne Booth. His reputation does not rest on the construction of a single theory in the way of a Stanley Fish or a Harold Bloom. Nor will he submit to the sponsorship of one particular institution. He has held chairs in universities provincial, metropolitan, ancient, and modern, so that there is something appropriate in a recent book jacket that describes him as "the retired King Edward VII Professor, currently dividing his time between Cambridge, London, and New York." Not for Kermode the fixed perspectives of Chicago, New Haven, or even Paris. By the same token, he has always eschewed fixed ideological commitments: the neo-Christianity that swept through the academy when he began has no more claim on his loyalty than have the various movements within it today.

This remarkably low level of doctrinal affiliation perhaps accounts for the fact that Kermode's professional sphere of influence remains narrower than his academic standing might suggest. A sampling of entries credited to contemporary critics in the *Citations Index* for 1984 and 1985 discloses that he merits a total of 173 entries, in comparison with the 267 notched up by Harold Bloom and the staggering 736 accumulated by Roland Barthes. It is hard, too, to think of any younger critic who is professedly a Kermode disciple. Where Bloom and Barthes have bequeathed their admirers a theory, or at the very least a vocabulary, and so made imitation a practical proposition, Kermode has left only a series of dauntingly virtuoso performances. It is difficult to imagine any younger critic with the verbal sophistication and the scholarly audacity needed to emulate *The Sense of an Ending* and *The Genesis of Secrecy*.

Nevertheless, it seems unfair to measure Kermode's true sphere of influence in these narrowly professional terms. For all his professed commitment to what he calls the "secret senses," he has continued to behave as a traditional man of letters. Perhaps the most puzzling paradox of this metaphysical critic's later career is that the great hierophant continues to write like the great communicator. How many contemporary critics could offer a more lucid account of current epistemological confusions than the penultimate chapter of *The Genesis of Secrecy*? In theory, these pages may well endorse a position of utter nihilism; but they do so in prose as persuasive and, ultimately, as conservative as Matthew Arnold's.

There are always plenty of candidates for the last romantic, but Kermode alone can claim Edmund Wilson's title as the last bookman. No other critic has Wilson's breadth. No other critic has his fluent lucidity. It is fascinating to imagine a cultural historian of the next century falling on either of them, to discover a series of nonaligned but passionate reflections on issues of pressing contemporary weight. But it is not just the future that owes a debt to Kermode. In his own century he has for nearly forty years kept open the lines of communication between the academy and the general public, and he has done so in a prose that continues to provide copious and elegant commentaries on matters of permanent intellectual concern.

NOTES

Notes to Chapter I: Introduction

1. *Continuities* (London: Routledge and Kegan Paul, 1968), 27. Cited hereafter as *CS* in text.

2. Jonathan Arac, "History and Mystery: The Criticism of Frank Kermode," *Salmagundi* 55 (1982): 135–55 (139); Gerald Graff, "Do It Yourself," *American Scholar* 45 (1976): 306–10 (308).

3. "The End of the World," *Listener*, 5 October 1967, 430–32 (431).

4. *In Defence of the Imagination* (Oxford: Clarendon Press, 1982), 112, 23.

5. *The Movement* (New York: Oxford University Press, 1980), 26.

6. *The Art of Telling* (Cambridge, Mass.: Harvard University Press, 1983), 54. Cited hereafter as *AT* in text.

7. "The Young and the Elders," *Partisan Review* 37 (1970): 184–98 (195).

8. "Do It Yourself," 307.

9. "Educating the Planet," *London Review of Books*, 20 March 1980, 1–4 (1).

10. "Figura," in *Scenes from the Drama of European Literature* (New York: Meridian Books, 1959), 11–76 (73).

11. *The Genesis of Secrecy* (Cambridge, Mass.: Harvard University Press, 1979), 122–23. Cited hereafter as *GS* in text.

12. *The Sense of an Ending* (New York: Oxford University Press, 1967), ix. Cited hereafter as *SE* in text.

13. "Coming Up for Air," *New York Review of Books*, 15 July 1976, 40–42 (42).

14. "The Enduring *Lear*," *New York Review of Books*, 12 May 1966, 12–14 (14).

Notes to Chapter II: The Image

1. "Spatial Form: An Answer to Critics," *Critical Inquiry* 4 (1977): 231–52 (242).

2. *Romantic Image* (London: Fontana Books, 1971), 181. Cited hereafter as *RI* in text.

3. "The Dancer and the Tree," *Times Literary Supplement*, 17 May 1957, 304–5 (304).

4. Review of *Romantic Image*, *Victorian Studies* 2 (1959): 75–77 (76).

5. "Common and Uncommon Muses," *Twentieth Century* 162: 458–68 (460).

6. "A Myth of Catastrophe," *Listener*, 8 November 1956, 745–46 (745).

7. Ibid., 745.

8. *The Finer Tone* (Baltimore: The Johns Hopkins Press, 1953), 3.

9. *Romanticism and the Modern Ego* (London: Martin Secker and Warburg, 1943), 24.

10. Foreword to *Critiques and Essays in Criticism, 1920–48*, edited by Robert Wooster Stallman (New York: Ronald Press, 1949), xv–xxii (xvi).

11. *The Poetry of Experience* (New York: W. W. Norton, 1963), 9, 27.

12. *The Poetic Image* (London: Jonathan Cape, 1947), 17, 35.

13. *Poetical Works*, edited by Ernest de Selincourt (London: Oxford University Press, 1969), 737.

14. Stallman, *Critiques*, 488–90; Edmund Wilson, "T. S. Eliot and the Church of England," in *The Shores of Light* (London: W. H. Allen, 1952), 436–41; Yvor Winters, *In Defense of Reason* (Chicago: Swallow Press, 1947), 411; Bonamy Dobrée, "The Claims of Sensibility," *Humanitas* 1 (1946): 55–58; F. W. Bateson, "Contributions to a Dictionary of Critical Terms. II. Dissociation of Sensibility," *Essays in Criticism* 1 (1951): 302–12 (307).

15. Graham Hough, "Symbolists and Moderns," *Encounter*, October 1957, 72–75 (74); Philip Larkin, Review in *Manchester Guardian*, 23 July 1957, 4; Thom Gunn, review in *London Magazine*, February 1958, 62–65.

16. *Meditations on a Hobby Horse* (Oxford: Phaidon Press, 1963), 82.

17. "The Metaphysical Poets," in *Selected Essays* (London: Faber and Faber, 1934), 281–91 (287).

18. Abrams, 77; Frank, 243.

19. "Notes on Language and Style," in *Further Speculations*, edited by Sam Hynes (Minneapolis: University of Minnesota Press, 1955), 86.

Notes to Chapter III: Fictions

1. *The Visionary Company* (New York: Anchor Books, 1963), xiv.

2. *Shakespeare, Spenser, Donne* (London: Routledge and Kegan Paul, 1971), 267. Cited hereafter as *SSD* in text.

3. *Puzzles and Epiphanies* (London: Routledge and Kegan Paul, 1962), 69. Cited hereafter as *PE* in text.

4. "Between Two Galaxies," *Encounter*, February 1963, 76–82 (81).

5. *The Two Cultures and A Second Look* (Cambridge: Cambridge University Press, 1964), 11.

6. "The Significance of C. P. Snow," *Spectator*, 9 March 1962, 297–303 (299).

7. *Beyond Culture* (New York: Harcourt Brace Jovanovich, 1978), 4.

8. "Strange Contemporaries," *Encounter*, May 1967, 65–69 (67).

9. Graham Hough, "The End of the World," *Listener*, 5 October

1967, 431; Christopher Ricks, "Fictions and Their Status," *Kenyon Review* 29 (1967): 555–61 (558).

10. J. R. Oppenheimer, "The Age of Science, 1900–1950," *Scientific American*, September 1950, 22.

11. *Poetries and Sciences* (New York: W. W. Norton, 1970), 48.

12. *Meditations on a Hobby Horse* (Oxford: Phaidon Press, 1963), 51.

13. "A High-Toned Old Christian Woman," in *The Collected Poems of Wallace Stevens* (London: Faber and Faber, 1955), 59; "About One of Marianne Moore's Poems," in *The Necessary Angel* (New York: Vintage Books, 1951), 93–103 (101–102).

14. Cited in H. Vaihinger, *The Philosophy of "As If,"* translated by C. K. Ogden (London: Kegan Paul, 1924), 344.

15. *Meditations on a Hobby Horse,* 82–83.

16. *The Philosophy "As If,"* 12–13 and 2, respectively.

17. *Meditations on a Hobby Horse,* 85.

18. "Reading Shakespeare's Mind," *New York Review of Books,* 12 October 1967, 14–17 (15, 17).

Notes to Chapter IV: The Classic

1. *Forms of Attention* (Chicago: University of Chicago Press, 1985), xiii. Cited hereafter as *FA* in text.

2. Charles-Augustin Sainte-Beuve, *Qu'est-ce qu'un classique?* (Heidelberg: Carl Winter, 1946), 7; "Preface to Shakespeare," in *Johnson on Shakespeare,* vols. 7 and 8 of *The Yale Editon of the Works of Samuel Johnson,* edited by Arthur Sherbo (New Haven: Yale University Press, 1968), 60–61.

3. "What is a Classic?" in *On Poetry and Poets* (London: Faber and Faber, 1957), 53–71 (61–62).

4. *Qu'est-ce qu'un classique?,* 11.

5. "Preface to Shakespeare," 62.

6. "What is a Classic?," 67–68.

7. *Qu'est-ce qu'un classique?,* 15.

8. "Survival of the Classics," *Encounter,* November 1963, 82–85 (85); "Marvell Transprosed," *Encounter,* November 1966, 77–84 (80).

9. *Sur Racine* (Paris: Éditions du Seuil, 1963), 149.

10. "Hierarchies Reconsidered," *Listener,* 23 August 1973, 248; "The Young and the Elders," *Partisan Review* 37 (1970): 195, 197–98.

11. "Reading Shakespeare's Mind," *New York Review of Books,* 12 October 1967, 14, 15.

12. "Lear at Lincoln Center," *New York Review of Books,* 25 June 1964, 4–5 (5).

13. "What is a Classic?," 55.

14. *The Classic* (Cambridge, Mass.: Harvard University Press, 1983), 140. Cited hereafter as *C* in text.

15. *The House of the Seven Gables*, edited by William Charvat, et al. (Ohio: Ohio State University Press, 1965), 276.

Notes to Chapter V: Interpretation

1. Oliver Taplin, "A Surplus of Signifier," *Essays in Criticism* 26 (1976): 339–45 (339); Quentin Anderson, "Classical Landscapes," *Times Literary Supplement*, 2 April 1976, 371; Gerald Graff, "Do It Yourself," *American Scholar* 45 (1976): 308.

2. Ralph Cohen, "A Note on *New Literary History*," *New Literary History* 1 (1969): 3–6 (4, 5).

3. Sheldon Sacks, "A Chimera for a Breakfast," *Critical Inquiry* 1 (1974): iii–vi (iii–iv).

4. (Oxford: Phaidon Press, 1963), ix.

5. "The Death of the Author," in *Image-Music-Text*, translated by Stephen Heath (Glasgow: Fontana, 1977), 142–48 (147).

6. "In Parvo," *Listener*, 12 October 1967, 474; "The Structures of Fiction," *Modern Language Notes* 84 (1969): 891–915 (891).

7. "Structuralism Domesticated," *London Review of Books*, 24 August 1981, 17.

8. Denis Donoghue, "Critical Response: A Reply to Frank Kermode," *Critical Inquiry* 1 (1974): 447–52 (447); Frank Kermode, "Sensing Endings," *Nineteenth Century Fiction* 33 (1978): 144–58 (158).

9. *The Gospel According to Saint Mark* (London: Macmillan, 1966), 472.

10. Quoted in R. P. C. Hanson, "Biblical Exegesis in the Early Church," in *The Cambridge History of the Bible*, vol. 1, edited by P. R. Ackroyd and C. F. Evans (Cambridge: Cambridge University Press, 1970), 412–53 (427).

11. Ibid., 436.

12. Ibid., 437.

13. *The Gospel According to Saint Mark*, 257 and 250, respectively.

14. Ibid., 257–58.

15. *A Study in Saint Mark* (London: Dacre Press, 1951), 7.

16. *The Practice of History* (Glasgow: Fontana Books, 1967), 88.

Notes to Chapter VI: Conclusion

1. "Novels about Adultery," *London Review of Books*, 15 May 1980, 1–3 (2, 3).

2. "The Decline of the Man of Letters," *Partisan Review* 52 (1985): 195–209 (209).

3. "T.V. Dinner," *New York Review of Books*, 20 August 1964, 15–16 (16).

4. *In Defense of Reason* (Chicago: Swallow Press, 1947), 466.

SELECTED WORKS BY FRANK KERMODE

Critical Works

Romantic Image. London: Routledge; New York: Macmillan, 1957.

Wallace Stevens. Edinburgh: Oliver and Boyd, 1960; New York: Grove Press, 1961. Revised edition, 1967.

Puzzles and Epiphanies: Essays and Reviews 1958–1961. London: Routledge; New York: Chilmark Press, 1962.

The Sense of an Ending: Studies in the Theory of Fiction. New York: Oxford University Press, 1967.

Continuities. London: Routledge; New York: Random House, 1968.

Shakespeare, Spenser, Donne: Renaissance Essays. London: Routledge; New York: Viking Press, 1971.

D. H. Lawrence. London: Fontana; New York: Viking Press, 1975.

The Classic. London: Faber; New York: Viking Press, 1975.

The Genesis of Secrecy. Cambridge, Mass.: Harvard University Press, 1979.

Essays on Fiction, 1971–1982. London: Routledge; published in the United States as *The Art of Telling: Essays on Fiction*. Cambridge, Mass.: Harvard University Press, 1983.

Forms of Attention. Chicago: University of Chicago Press, 1985.

Critical Editions

Editor, *English Pastoral Poetry: From the Beginnings to Marvell*. London: Harrap; New York: Barnes and Noble, 1952.

Editor, *The Tempest*, by William Shakespeare. London: Methuen, 1954.

Editor, *Seventeenth Century Songs*. London: Oxford University Press, 1956.

Editor, *The Living Milton: Essays by Various Hands*. London: Routledge, 1960; New York: Macmillan, 1961.

Editor, *Discussions of John Donne*. Boston: Heath, 1962.

Editor, *Spenser: Selections from the Minor Poems and the Faerie Queene*. London: Oxford University Press, 1965.

Editor, *Four Centuries of Shakespearean Criticism*. New York: Avon, 1965.

Editor, *The Metaphysical Poets: Essays on Metaphysical Poetry*. Greenwich, Conn.: Fawcett, 1969.

General Editor, *Modern Masters*. London: Fontana Collins, 1969–; New York: Viking Press, 1970–.

Editor, *King Lear: A Casebook*. London: Macmillan, 1969; Nashville: Aurora Publishers, 1970.

Editor, with Richard Poirier, *The Oxford Reader: Varieties of Contemporary Discourse*. New York: Oxford University Press, 1971.

General Editor, with John Hollander and others, *The Oxford Anthology of English Literature*. New York: Oxford University Press, 1973.

Editor, *Selected Prose of T. S. Eliot*. London: Faber; New York: Harcourt Brace-Farrar Straus, 1975.

General Editor, *The Oxford Authors Series*. Oxford: Oxford University Press, 1984–.